It is Coming

*What Jesus Really Said About
The End of the Age*

A Study of Jesus' Olivet Discourse
As recorded in *Mark 13, Matthew 24* and *Luke 21*
In the light shed by recognizing the Validity And Authority of
Matthew 24:9 and *Luke 21:12*

It is easy to understand and
you may very well see it.

This is no dream.

Fourth Edition

For more information about this book
And other writings about the Soon Return of Jesus
Please visit www.itiscoming.com

Marantha
Betty and Bob Gibson
604 E Market Ave
Searcy, AR 72143
(501) 268-4021
bobandbettygibson@gmail.com

Table of Contents

Foreword

Dear kind and gentle reader,

What if in your mid years, while sorting through some very old records you discovered to your total amazement and dismay that you had been adopted as an infant. That your mother and daddy weren't really your parents and that your brothers and sisters weren't really your siblings. That your name wasn't really your name and that the forebears of the stories you had been told really weren't your forebears. That even your nationality was not what you thought it was. How would you feel? Let me venture to say that you would feel disconnected.

Perhaps when you finish reading this story you will have an idea of what it is to experience such feelings.

However, what if further searching revealed to you that you, in fact, were descended from supreme royalty and belonged to the most ancient and exalted family in all of history. Certainly then you would quickly depart from grieving your disconnectedness. You would pass quickly through a silent rage at those who had kidnapped you and held you captive in ignorance all of those years. You would move rapidly on in a determined effort to seize the glory that was rightfully yours.

But only by your forgiving the evil deeds of others committed against you in ignorance and by your own accepting from God forgiveness for your own complicity, will you be free from this past to move on. You know in your heart that you are truly an accomplice because you failed to live up to the glory of your true genetics even though you had been ignorant of them.

By offering and accepting this interdependent forgiveness, this inseparably coupled Forgiveness of others by you and you by God, oh sweet gift of God, God soothes and comforts you and calms your resentment.

Giving and receiving this mercy frees you from the failure and bondage of the past to turn with all your heart and to address with all your might the recovery of the blessings lost to the years of the locust.

A very pointed story from *God to you* told with very short strokes is to be found in what follows.

The rambling and apparent repetition that you might find here is not principally a contrivance to emphasize a point, but is a direct result of seeking *you*. I desperately want to find *you* and sit down with *you* and tell *you* this story *from God* face-to-face, heart-to-heart. But *you* are many. *Your heart* is in a thousand different spiritual places and knows a thousand different spiritual languages.

O, how can I reach your heart?

You see, *you* are my family that adopted me, provided for me, fed me and cared for me while I was but a helpless babe. This story is especially for *you*. You are also that descendent part of the family that has often looked back in vain for guidance. *This story is for you. Forgive.*

You are also the church that nurtured and instructed me and told me the stories of the past. *This story is also for you. O, how I hope you can hear it.*

You are scores of missionaries and dozens of professors and student preachers debating into the night things very imperfectly understood by all. *This story is especially for YOU. Please find it.*

You are also the half a hundred prophecy authors and lecturers who face-to-face and by books, magazines, tapes, videos and seminars have encouraged and instructed us. This story is *especially for you. Please read it. I know that most of you will, for you are seekers. There is strong evidence that you have not yet fully comprehended the impact of the truth that is presented here.*

You are all of the kith and kin and the familiar.

But you are also the foreigner and the stranger.

You are the teacher brought to interpret for the foreigners in the Mongolian mining camp, clutching tightly to your chest the old worn out New Testament that would be the only English text available to your students for next year's instruction. *This story is for you, but how shall I start and how shall I proceed that you might hear?*

You were also in the circle of eager young men with open hearts and open Bibles, sheltered from the roaring wind in the gun tub on ship in mid-Atlantic so innocently, so intently, and yet steeped in so much ignorance, seeking *His will. This story is also for you. But how shall I begin?*

You are the Catholic priest of the Canadian order of the White Fathers sharing shelter and tea, discussing the sad division of God's people and the impact of the recently concluded Vatican II, while your acolyte and Grandwell debate baptism in Kiswahili before the village now gathered in your chapel, sheltered from the tropical downpour that had interrupted our outdoor evangelism and which now contended for a third position in that debate with its roar upon the corrugated roof. *This story is for you. I know you can hear, if I can but speak the language of your heart.*

You are the Muslim truck driver baptized in the Med at midnight with your best shoes on and a full pack of cigarettes in your shirt pocket. *This story is for you.*

You are the bright young Yugoslav Midshipman who, while reflecting on the fact that you had fallen in love, suddenly realized that there had to be more to life than that which was encompassed by the dialectic materialism regurgitated by your professors. It dawned on you that if ethereal love exists and is real, there also must be *God* just like your grandmother had always said. *This story is for you wherever you are.*

You are the Cossack Colonel of Ballistic Missiles, whose job in the Soviet Union was to target U. S. cities, who held hands and bowed your head in prayer to the *God* above, in a circle of love and devotion with those whom you had targeted, and may some day target again, *God* forbid. *This story is also for You. I know you will understand.*

You are the shy young Chinese doctor on Bellaire, handing out your Falon Gong pamphlets written in a language you can barely speak, but with eyes that shine with the universal longing for the reality of *God. This story is for you.*

You are the dear lost and very displaced Egyptian mechanic standing in the driveway at midnight declaring your manhood that you said would ultimately be demonstrated by standing boldly before *God* at Judgment and taking responsibility for your own sins and not wimping out like Christians, laying it all off on Jesus. *O, This story is for you.*

You were among the ones seen wandering among the graves and in the monuments to the dead of the Christian Wars in Hamburg, Ulm, St. Paul's and Melbourne, The Punch bowl, Tobruk, St. Petersburg, Moscow and countless American Civil War battlefields and wondering if Jesus had anything more to say about these matters than those scriptures with which both sides so often praised their dead, *"Greater love has no one than this, than to lay down one's life for his friends". This story is for you.*

You are the dear Jews, the dear Muslims, the dear Sikhs and Hindus, the dear polygamists, and your dear wives, dear communists and dear humanists, classmates, shipmates, coworkers neighbors and foreigners, here and abroad by the thousands that I have known and *should have loved* as *Jesus* does. *This story is for you.*

But dear friend, *you* are especially *the one* never met, never known. The very pointed story which follows, which is written with very short strokes is *especially for you.* But you will have to find it for yourself, because it lies mingled among all the other very short stories I have tried to address to all the others to whom a great debt is also owed. Please be patient with me. When you find it, *you* will know that it is *your story, your story that is truly from God and is truly for you.*

Your story is from *God*, but it comes to you in a vessel of clay. This shoddy jar is a broken clay pot, not comely to behold and not easy to handle, but within it is the priceless treasure of The Word of God. And it is for you.

However, thank *God*, the *fundamental impact* of this story as it speaks to you, will not depend upon the style of its telling nor primarily upon your hearing either, but rather, it will rest in the most absolute terms upon the *Word of God* that is in it and upon *The Holy Spirit* that opens the human heart to hear the *Word of God.*

This story is not a treatise, but an entreaty. It is much more a passion of the heart than an activity of the mind. The issues it addresses are certainly not the only quarrels we have with the devil. And it does not directly deal with the closest call we will have with hell. Certainly, personal sin, concealed, unconfessed and not repented of, is that. But it does deal with one of the broadest and most institutionalized attacks with which we must contend and one of the most severe challenges to our faith that we will ever face. And the time is very short.

You may be tempted to ask yourself over and over again *"Where have I been?"* When you find *your story* from *God.* Instead let the overriding state of your mind not be a question at all, but rather, a shout of praise bursting from a heart overflowing with joy and expectation.

May The God of all glory and of all comfort richly bless you.

Introduction

It is Coming is not fiction. It is the *true story* of a *battle* that has been raging across the face of the earth and heavens for millennia between the Prince of Peace, and the prince of darkness of this present world. This is a *colossal battle* with unimaginable hordes of spirit creatures, singular and in vast array, slipping surreptitiously through the darkness and charging with raging tumult at high noon. *This is a battle to the death* or to *life*. The story of the battle is a Trilogy with its volumes being *past*, *present* and *future*.

The battle rages today and it is now nearing its cataclysmic finale. We are in the midst of the conflict. The weapons at our disposal are truth, faith, hope and love. The enemy's weapon is deception, deception and deception and all of the evil, horror, death and destruction that follow in its wake.

It is Coming is *nonfiction*. You are *a main character* in the story. The story is not over. What yet remains of the story, which is its climactic finale, *is in our immediate future*. And this, *our future,* is also a real life story. In fact it is no story at all. *It is the starkest of reality and it is coming. The final chapter is at the door.*

You see the Scriptures tell us that the Messiah would come from the root of *Jesse*, but the Scriptures also say that Jesse's son, King David, called him Lord! The scribes wondered how this could possibly be. Why would David call one of his remote descendants Lord?

And just as astounding is the declaration in Isaiah 9 that the whole world will call a child, *Mighty God!* *"For unto us a child is born, unto us a son is given and the government will be upon His shoulder, and His name will be called wonderful, counselor, Mighty God, Everlasting Father, Prince of Peace. Of the increase of His government and peace there will be no end, upon the throne of David and over his kingdom, to order it and establish it with judgment and justice from that time forward, even forever. The zeal of the Lord of Hosts will perform this."*

Right here, seven hundred years before Jesus was born, Isaiah plainly reveals that, Messiah, Prince of Peace, Root of Jesse and Lord of David is mighty God, Everlasting Father. Maybe the scribes can't understand it, or simply can't stand it, but that is what the Scriptures say. Now also in Isaiah 46, Almighty God who is also Everlasting Father declares, *"Remember the former things of old, for I am God and there is no other; I am God, and there is none like Me, declaring the end from the beginning, and from ancient times things that are not yet done..."*

Mighty God, Everlasting Father said that there was *no* one like Him, that *He Alone* could foretell the end from the beginning. Although He sent many prophets many times to tell the future, none of them was granted the full vision to plainly tell the story to the very end. He reserved this very special show of divine power for Himself so that He could forcefully demonstrate especially to the final generation who *He really is in the flesh*, to give them one final proof and one last chance.

This terminal generation will be full of scoffers and of doubt, but as it witnesses the unfolding of the events of the end some will recognize that they are seeing exactly what was foretold and they will remember who foretold it. Then they will have the final data in their hands, confirming the identity of the Messiah, Prince of Peace, Mighty God, Everlasting Father, the Only One who told the end from the beginning and the Only One whom they can trust for their salvation.

Then those who will be saved will know that Jesus of Nazareth, root of Jesse, descendant of David, is also Lord of David, Messiah, Prince of Peace, and *Mighty God, Everlasting Father*, because they will remember that, *on the Mount of Olives in His last hours almost two thousand years ago Jesus plainly foretold the history of the world from His day in the flesh to the very end and that this is the sign that God reserved for Himself alone.* Even now, we know this will happen because all of the things that Jesus said on the Mount of Olives would happen, have happened, just as He said they would, even to this very generation!

Because of this, the truth lovers of the terminal generation should have no problem in recognizing *Him as Mighty God, Everlasting Father.* Current events and all history leading up to them will unfold, just as *He* foretold that they would, before their wondering eyes to establish *His* credentials and prove *His* claim. To *Him* they can turn for their salvation.

However, very sadly our adversary, the grandmaster of deception, who is the very father of all falsehood has managed, by his wiles, to confuse the minds of most generations about what *Jesus really said on the Mount of Olives.*

As a result, perception has been muddled. Clarity on this issue is gone and the storyline that Jesus gave us has been lost. Consequently, the *Gospel Record* of what *Jesus actually said on the Mount of Olives* has been discounted for many years, and still is, simply as allegory by most people. This terrible situation was brought about by the deceiver so that those, especially, of the last generation who are fooled by this deception will be deprived in the very hour of their greatest need of the final and absolute proof of His identity as Mighty God, Everlasting Father, and their Savior. *They will also miss the season of His return, and His instructions for their escape.*

In the meantime, this deadly and very tenacious deception has already brought massive havoc, death and destruction on all of the intervening generations.

You see, if the prophecy is muddled in its telling and retelling, then its fulfillment in history and current life will pass unnoticed and its Author will pass unrecognized and unhonored. That is exactly what was intended by the foe and has, in fact, actually happened throughout History and especially is happening today.

It is Coming is the nonfiction account of this age old deception, how it was accomplished, what its consequences have been down through the ages and what a terrifying surprise it holds in store for the unsuspecting of this present generation who are now held in its thrall.

But the main purpose of *It Is Coming* is to rip off that veil of deception that the foe has cast over *the plain words which Jesus spoke on the Mount of Olives* so that the light of the knowledge of *His prophetic word* can shine on this present generation; so that *what God said in the Holy Scriptures may not be stolen from us and our children any longer*, so that Jesus, the bright and morning star of our life and our salvation, may rise more abundantly, even now in the hearts of this present generation, before it is too late.

Please read on and let the veil be ripped off and the plain light of day and the glory of His word shine in."*The secret things belong to the lord our God, but those things that are revealed belong to us and our children forever...*" *Deuteronomy 29:29*

The things that will come to your mind in *It Is Coming were plainly revealed to us by God through Jesus* almost two thousand years ago on the Mount of Olives, but they were hidden again and have been kept secret from us by the deception of Satan with the complicity of men for about the last seventeen hundred years.

"*For if they did not escape who refused Him who spoke on earth, much more shall we not escape if we turn away from Him who speaks from heaven.*" *Hebrews 12:23*

"*So we have the prophetic word confirmed, which you do well to heed as a light that shines in a dark place, until the day dawns and the morning star rises in your hearts.*" *II Peter 1:19*

"*Worship God for the testimony of Jesus is the spirit of prophecy.*" *Revelation 19:10*

Background and Synopsis

It Is Coming

> *"For He received from God the Father honor and glory when such a voice came to Him from the excellent glory, "This is My beloved Son, in whom I am pleased." And we heard this voice, which came from heaven when we were with Him on the holy mountain and so we have the prophetic word confirmed, which you do well to heed as a light that shines in a dark place, until the day dawns and the morning star rises in your hearts; knowing this first, that no prophecy of Scripture is of any private interpretation, for prophecy never came by the will of man, but holy men of God spoke as they were moved by the Holy Spirit."*
> *II Peter 1:17–21*

On the *Mount of Olives* in His last week in this flesh the Son of God *clearly foretold the history of the world*, beginning with the events that would occur in that very generation in which He lived in the flesh and continuing *to the very end of the age, to the very time in which we now live*. What *He* said on the mountain is recorded in three of the *Gospels*. The three gospel recorders were not eye or ear witnesses to these teachings of Jesus. But all three were chosen by *God* to do the work of recording and *inspired by the Holy Spirit of God* to do it right. Therefore, of course, what they clearly wrote that Jesus said would happen, has happened precisely as *they wrote that it would happen* ever since *they wrote it*. Only a very few events and a very short time remain before their foretold stories come to their end and this age draws to its close. Great blessings belong, especially to those of this generation, who read, understand and act upon what they wrote because the end of the age events clearly *foretold by Jesus* and *recorded by them* are now at hand.

These prophecies of Jesus which are in your Bible are clear to see and easy to understand, both in their telling and in their fulfillment, even by children, or maybe it should be said, especially by children.

God wants this generation, especially, to know what is going to happen next.

However, this plain foretelling of the history of the world by Jesus has been hidden from most of us for most of our lives by the schemes of our Adversary, who has labored mightily to obscure those Scriptures that tell the story so plainly so that we will be *blinded to the reality of what has been - and what is to come.*

Knowing this *first*, that no prophecy of Scripture is of any private interpretation, know this also that these three gospel authors wrote as they were moved by the Holy Spirit, just as surely as their God spoke from heaven. *Thus it is written.* (As recorded in Matthew, Mark & Luke) and *thus it has happened - so far* (As recorded in the history of the world, so far). A*nd thus we know it will happen even to the end of the age.*

We must not let Satan steal from us and our children any longer this foreknowledge of the future by continuing to lead us to discount (to effectively despise and disregard) the Scriptures that tell us so plainly the story that He so wants us to know.

To secure the blessings of these revelations of the Lord for our selves and our children we must know and understand the truth that God has delivered to us through these Holy Prophets at such great cost. We must wake up and listen to them to receive these blessings. We must also wake up and hear the lion roar.

"The secret things belong to the Lord our God, but those things that *are revealed* belong to us and our children forever,..."
Deuteronomy 29:29

It Is Coming is a wake up call. It is a light which shines on what Jesus said about the history of the world, the future of the world and the end of the age. Come and see. The night is far spent and the day is dawning.

It Is Coming is also a light which shines on the dark campaign of Satan, which he has conducted to obscure what Jesus said. Come and consider the dark prowling in the midst of the Church and among the Scriptures, of our ravenous adversary down though the centuries and into the present. Deeply ponder the lion's ways and let the hair bristle on the back of your neck as his silent presence turns into a roar.

Satan began this dark campaign only a few years after Jesus' departure. His attack has been pressed hard under an obscuring cloud of deception ever since and continues to this very day. The Adversary began this dark action by persuading the church leaders in very early centuries to effectively *change* what *Jesus actually said* on the Mount of Olives in His last week in the flesh.

Right there on the Mount of Olives Jesus clearly foretold the future of the world all of the way to the very end. There He also gave His final instructions to His disciples for the actions they were to take. Satan didn't then, and doesn't now, want us to know what Jesus really said and what Jesus meant for us to do about it.

By recasting the meaning of Jesus' teachings, Satan hoped that the Church, Israel and the whole world could be effectively blinded to their immediate future, to the whole course of human history and especially to the events of the end of the age, which Jesus had so clearly foretold there.

A very simple, but subtle strategy, was used by the Adversary to recast Jesus' teaching and to blind the world. It was to mix and mingle the three Gospel Accounts. The three accounts were repackaged and presented as simply three versions of a single short story, as if told from different perspectives, rather than different chapters of a comprehensive accounting of the remaining history of the world.

In the process of rolling all of the accounts together each account was forced to give up the distinctive vital details contained within it, which gives the overall story its coherence. In addition, this mingling of the accounts deprived each account of its own distinctive character, its authenticity and its own internal integrity.

In this process each author lost his credibility as a trustworthy Prophet chosen by God. In manhandling the Scriptures to make them fit one another, the church effectively elevated its authority above the Scriptures and above the Prophets.

The assumption of this authority by the church opened the floodgates to human editing of the Scriptures. Man supposed he could rewrite the future of the world simply by making adjustments to the Prophesies. Was this degradation of the Scriptures a result of this audacious action or was it a prerequisite for it? Or was it both?

This simultaneous mingling of accounts and elevation of the church above the Scriptures was accomplished by presenting the three accounts in a new light. The new presentation was that all three accounts were simply parallel attempts to record Jesus' descriptions of the very same then-coming events of the first century. This new view was that all three accounts were just retelling the very same, very short story, namely: *A Brief History of the First Century Church*, rather than clearly telling the distinctly different parts of a very much longer story, namely: The *Whole History of the World From That Day Until the End of the Age*, which is what the Scriptures plainly say that they do.

The worldly church saw a great advantage in doing the Devil's will by adjusting our understanding of these Scriptures to this new view. This adjustment would recast the teachings of Jesus, very much in their favor, as they saw it, as we shall see.

The Scriptures were tuned, not by actually changing the texts, but by reinterpreting them, by bending their meaning; sometimes slightly, sometimes violently, and even especially by ignoring them. The very awkward inconsistencies in the texts that inadvertently, but naturally, resulted from these sometimes pale and sometimes extravagant perversions, had to be muted and the rough edges rounded off for this new construct to hold together and to be somehow credible. This is what the harmonizing of the

Mount of Olives Discourse, which is found even in today's modern commentaries, is all about.

For example, in attempting to make all three records say consistent things about what was supposedly the same event, one of the Gospel Accounts was given the lead credibility in a given passage. Then the teaching of any other account, which showed up as a variant to the selected passage was forced to conform to the selected passage. Then all accounts would be made to appear to be saying consistent things about supposedly the same event.

Sometimes this was easy and sometimes it was a stretch. An example of a stretch is where the *Abomination of Desolation standing in the Holy Place* of **Matthew 24:15** had to be equated to *armies encircling Jerusalem of Luke 21:20* as the sign to flee to the Mountains of Judea before the desolation of Jerusalem. These two descriptions had to be interpreted as describing the same single event for the harmony to hold. Of course, major contortions of Scripture, history, thought and logic ensued from this effort.

In some cases the words of the texts just couldn't be made to conform at all and the whole variant phrase had to be abandoned completely in the teaching to make the harmony hold. In these cases, the offending phrase was just ignored. It just disappeared altogether. It vanished! *No, not from the page, but from the teachings.* Those well schooled in this hermeneutic today can read right past a phrase without even having it register in their minds. Understanding this phenomenon gives insight into the term *brainwashing*.

The prime example of this is the failed necessity of making the essential event-sequencing word, *"before"* of *Luke 21:12* mean the same thing as the word, *"then"* i.e. *"after"* of *Matthew 24:9*. Since these verses cannot, in any way, be reconciled, the full force of the Harmony hermeneutic had to be brought to bear. The harmonizers just abandoned the reading of *Luke* altogether in favor of *Matthew* for this particular phrase in their teaching.

This is when a word or phrase literally became invisible to the fully indoctrinated student. Those who write unigospels, or Jesus

Biographies even today, under the sway of the harmonizers have to choose one text over the other. They cannot be harmonized.

In order to make their scheme work they accepted Matthew's "version" for these two particular verses in their teaching and abandon God's word in Luke, as if it counted for nothing and meant nothing. All of this was done simply because of the *a priori* assumption that the three accounts were just trying to relate the same tale and merely got their words wrong.

This whole process is, of course, diametrically opposed to *hearing* The Word Of God. Instead of *listening to God*, in their picking and choosing they were editing, correcting and censoring *God's* Prophets. They were, in effect, taking *God's* place and rewriting *His Word*. How they had abandoned their faith and their fear of *God*! But we see this phenomenon in our very own day, probably in our very own hearts, if we would dare look close enough. As weird and frightening as this is, it happens.

How could such a strategy as harmonizing away the truth possibly work? It would certainly have to be done over time in silent conspiracy by powerful, deceived and maybe morally compromised men. These leaders, like the religious rulers in Jesus' day, would have to consider their own opinions and judgments above the *Scriptures* and *Their Author.* Like the Pharisees they would have certainly cared little for the folk that would be mislead into eternity by their terrible misdeeds.

It would also certainly have required the acquiescence of a trusting, passive and sleeping pew, a people who had been lulled into carelessly turning over their priceless inheritance of God's Eternal Word and Eternal Life to the safe keeping of others. It would basically require a *non-believing* church.

It would take time. It wouldn't be done over night. It probably wasn't done without great strife. But it really isn't difficult to understand that it could be done, even at this remote time, what with the recent example of the Sodomy Party of the Episcopalian Church staring us in the face.

In summary, The basic false premise that was seized upon to fundamentally adjust the church's thinking about what Jesus really said was that all three accounts were describing the same events in this foretold history of the world, despite the fact that *Jesus* plainly taught in *Luke 21:12* and *Matthew 24:9* that they are not. This basic premise forced The Harmonizers to disregard *Luke 21:12* altogether because of *Matthew 24:9*

With this malfeasance in place they were then able to apply *Matthew's* Account as well as *Luke's* Account to the events of the first century only. And this was probably their main purpose in the first place.

This misappropriation of Scripture obscured the entire story that Jesus told on The Mount of Olives.

This reconstructing of ***God's Prophetic Word*** was done in total disregard of the declaration of the sovereignty of ***God's Word*** as given through His Prophets which is found in ***II Peter 1:17-21***. That is why ***This Background and Synopsis*** of ***It Is Coming*** begins with ***These Verses from Second Peter***. Please turn back and read them once again.

The major impact of this blending of the Gospel Records was to make it appear as if both Matthew and Luke were covering the same prophetic ground and that, therefore, there was only one destruction of Jerusalem foretold by Jesus on the Mount of Olives and that it occurred in 70 AD.

According to this new construct, ***all*** that ***Matthew Recorded*** relating to the end times, also took place in 70 AD.

The immediate and probably the primary intended impact of this new doctrine was to give credence to the theory that Israel had been foreclosed on and replaced by the Church in all of the special promises of Power, Dominion and Salvation that God had made specifically to Israel in *Both Testaments*. The timing in Church History of the advent of this new doctrine strongly supports this probability. The huge impact of this doctrine on history and our present thinking will be addressed later.

And although it may not have been the primary goal, a catastrophic collateral consequence of this misapplication of *Matthew's Account* to the events 70 AD is that it stripped *The New Testament* of the only clear historically reliable account concerning the real last days, which is what *Matthew's Account* is really all about. If the authority, certainty, specificity and clarity of *Jesus' teachings in Matthew 24* can be removed, it is child's play to manhandle *John's* record of *Jesus'* later *Revelation*. And that is exactly what has been done.

Those who have bought in to the harmonizers reconstruction of Jesus' Olivet Discourse have been on their own for nearly 2000 years and are even now stumbling headlong into the darkness without a light.

As a final injury, this muddling of *The Foretelling of World History by Jesus on the Mount Of Olives* has robbed this present doubting generation, as they are making life's most important decision, of the opportunity to consider one of Jesus' most important credentials as *The Messiah and their Savior.*

It Is Coming is an attempt to unveil this error. If you are a Bible believer and will persevere, this investigation should be able to unveil this error to you. Even if you have doubts about the Bible's authority and accuracy, please persevere. What you read here may very well change your mind even about that, and change it altogether.

Sadly, most Bible Expositors down through the centuries have followed the Early Father's harmonizing, apparently without significant reservation, and have upheld *These Traditional Teachings* of what, by their time, was (and still is) The *well-established Orthodox Doctrine of the Church,*

However, *in the process Jesus' Mount of Olives teachings have been totally obscured, including the foretold history of the world, God's plan for the Jews in this history, and the approaching end of the age. And, again, another extraordinary result is that one of the most convincing evidences that Jesus is assuredly the Son of the Living God has also been hidden.*

This obfuscation has subtly, effectively and fundamentally altered who *Jesus* was and what *He* taught in the minds of many. Was this done on purpose? It would seem that, on the human plane, the intent of some of the earliest expositors might very well have been to conceal at least one of these vital truths. The very best that can be said of the continued silencing of these

Scriptures throughout the ages, a silencing that continues to this very day, of *These* and other related *Scriptures*, especially *Romans 9, 10 & 11* is that it is most likely done in steeped, ingrained and perhaps, totally invisible (*brainwashed*) ignorance.

This present exposition, which is now in your hands, rests *solely* on faith in *God* and in *His desire, intention and ability to express Himself to us through His Holy Spirit in His chosen Prophets.* Here there is no suppression of what may appear, at first observation, to be mistakes made by *The Recording Prophets.* Instead, what at first may appear to be mistakes in *The Scriptures*, are taken rather as challenges to our own very limited vision and very limited understanding to humble us, to be prayed over and to be a blessed occasion for waiting upon *God.* They are not taken as *Challenges To God's Competence* to be corrected by us, as the ancient expositors must have thought that it was their duty and prerogative to do.

The story you are about to read is very old, but most likely, you have not heard it yet. If it is new to you, as you try to cope with it, you will probably labor under an immense burden of preconceptions built by centuries of orthodox teaching. If you persevere you will discover, however, that these ancient accepted teachings sadly rest more directly on the *traditions of men* than on the *Word of God*.

> *We must love the Lord, our God, more than we love what we have been taught by men or the truth will escape us even now.*

The main body of *This Expose'* which follows further develops all of the issues covered in this *Background And Synopsis.* It explores the impact of the twisting of Jesus' Olivet teaching on the church, its doctrines, and its actions, and on world history, current events and those yet to come.

We will see that the fruit of this campaign of deception has dominated major aspects of Church doctrine and action for the last 1700 years. And that its influence over the church in ages past and in this present age is literally beyond human calculation and very sadly is still mainly beyond human recognition and comprehension.

It Is Coming also explores possible motives and agendas and known horrific results of this twisting of these Scriptures. Further, it examines, *Chapters 9,10* and *11* of *Paul's letter to the Romans* as the silencing of these chapters relates to the silencing of *Luke 21:12*. We will see how this broad censorship has lead to *The Altered Conceptions of: Jesus and His Teachings, the Church, the Jewish Nation* and *the End of the Age*, which have so engulfed the saints through the ages.

It Is Coming also explores the impact of the truth on our generation of what Jesus actually said about coming events and their order and duration, including: *the Rapture, the Tribulation and what we should be doing right now.*

It Is Coming, however, first indulges in a very personal story in an urgent attempt to capture your attention (just as mine was when I was so drastically jerked to a stop and turned around by the *Word of God*) and to focus it on the vital issues that now lie in our immediate future.

May our God and Father and Jesus, Our Savior, Lord and Brother, Who is Coming for His own very soon, Bless you richly *So that you may fully trust Him until He comes* and being filled with the Holy Spirit, *rise to meet Him in the air when He comes.*
Maranatha

The Astounding Anomaly of the Gospels

A Well–Kept Secret
Makes for a Startling Surprise
(A Very Personal Story)

The Conundrum

I ask *you*, dear believer in the Word of God, what if *you* found *two completely different and profoundly contradicting teachings of our Lord and Savior Jesus, the Christ, in the Gospel accounts of Matthew and Luke?*

What would *you* think, especially if the time and setting of these two teachings were identical? The audience was the same. The circumstances were the same. The speaker was the Lord, Himself. And the subject of *His* teaching was of *utmost importance* to those who heard *Him* then and to those who read these two totally differing records today. These two records of His teachings are not just different, they are diametrically opposed. What confusion! What consternation of heart!

What would *you* think and what would *you* do?

I pray, Dear Believer, that *you* would not lose your faith, but rather, that your *curiosity* would be mightily aroused and your *attention* mightily focused.

The Experience

This is exactly what happened to me. And this is the story of what I thought and what I did and what *I am still learning from this experience.*

1

I was an elder and had been a Bible teacher for forty years in a church that was very dear to me, a church that my family had belonged to, at least since the days of my great-grandfather. My earliest and fondest childhood memories were of the church. Its teachings, directly from the pulpit and the sand table and through every family relationship, were the foundation of my understanding, of my belief, of my very life. I loved the church. Although flawed by some of its people and perhaps by some of its actions, its precepts and doctrines were perfect and stainless. Of this I had no doubt.

The church was committed to the noble concept of the restoration of New Testament Christianity. We believed that the Bible, with special emphasis on the New Testament, was our only and all sufficient guide to the restoration of first century Christianity and in all matters of life and doctrine. I believed in the inerrancy of the Word of God, both the Old and New Testaments. Dearly beloved, I still do.

Then several years ago, my wife and older son challenged me to undertake a personal in-depth study of the *Book of Revelation*, a book I knew little about, in spite of my many years as a teacher in the church.

They urged me over a period of several years to really study *The Revelation of Jesus Christ* because they had read Hal Lindsey's book, *The Late Great Planet Earth*. They had never before heard anything like what Hal had to say about the Rapture and the Tribulation. But they thought he was right. They lovingly and steadfastly persisted in their petition that I read Hal's book and really study *The Revelation*.

I resisted their imploring for several years because I knew that Lindsey was a *Pre-millenialist*. I believed that this was a heresy. In the church, my generation and I were of the *A-millenialist* persuasion. I believed this is what the Bible taught. *A-millenialism* was taken to be the rational and historically orthodox position, inherited from the church's ancient fathers. I was sure that it was *rooted* in *The Scriptures*. It was an unquestioned tradition.

2

Although not specifically found in The Scriptures, the a-millenial position had been endorsed by Augustine and other ancient fathers. By the fourth century, it was firmly established by the church as the orthodox view of how the world would end. And it was so simple. You know, it is appointed unto man once to die and after that the judgment.

This orthodoxy being accepted by Calvin and Luther had been faithfully transmitted through the reformation and the restoration to those who had taught me. Being a pragmatist, I believed it was a waste of good time to even study the issue since I accepted a-millenial to mean none or no millenium, which I believed was correct and was so simple. Why study that which doesn't even exist, just because some misled people thought that it did. It didn't seem to make much sense to spend time and energy in that direction. One less thing to worry about.

This rationale was wonderfully reinforced by the difficulty I had always faced in comprehending any part of *The Revelation* past Chapter 3 anyway. In my youthful forays, I had faithfully consulted with the several usual Protestant commentaries and Restoration Movement study guides. They all agreed that many learned men had various opinions about what all the symbolism meant. However, since the primary thrust of *The Revelation*, they said was to encourage the believers who lived way back in the first dark days of the persecuted church, any reasonable interpretation of the details was indifferently and totally acceptable for today's purposes.

It was believed that *The Book of Revelation* was intended for the early generations of the church, which would undergo fierce persecution at the hands of the state. It was said to have been written to encourage them not to give up the faith and it did so by presenting the final triumph of the faithful in extravagant and glorious symbolism. On the way, some of the symbolism even served as codes, employed to protect the believers by confusing their adversaries. For example, it contained references to Babylon, which was understood to really mean Rome.

We were faintly encouraged to read it for its insights into the apocalyptic style and for whatever encouragement we might receive from it as an inspirational reading in our own day.

With this kind of faint encouragement, practical busy people with real life problems didn't spend much time in *The Revelation*.

All this, in spite of the wonderfully singular promise of blessings to those who read, and those who hear, and *keep* the words of this Prophecy, a promise which is *absolutely unique* in all the New Testament and which applies specifically and uniquely to this writing alone!

When the Sunday School curriculum demanded an annual once through of the whole New Testament, the Revelation was always shorted.

Never-the-less, with interest growing in the church over End-Times teaching, the family's continued insistence that I read Hal's book took on new significance. However, as an alternative, I determined to tackle *The Book of Revelations* itself again, unaided. I certainly preferred to study *The Scriptures*, themselves, as difficult as I found them to be, rather than some man's book, especially from a man of known heretical views.

Then someone told me that Jesus' Olivet Discourse, which is recorded in the Gospels of *Matthew*, *Mark* and *Luke* was the "Little Apocalypse." That sounded very attractive to me, like the *Minor Prophets*, a quick study.

It also sounded perfectly safe. I had always been encouraged to read the Gospels. I often did, although my favorite Scriptures were *Paul's Epistles*, *Hebrews*, and the writings of *James* and *John*. As for the many things in *Paul's Epistles* that I didn't understand, I was comforted by Peter's personal appraisal of the difficulty of Paul's writings. If Peter had difficulty with understanding Paul, why should I suffer embarrassment if I couldn't understand or explain him either? As a result, I didn't push the hard parts.

Yes, I knew that Jesus had some hard sayings, too, but nobody ever told me that they were hard to understand, just hard to do. So I decided to look at what *He* had to say about the End-Times, in His own personal condensed form, in His "Little Apocalypse" in the Gospels before tackling the big one in *The Revelation.*

So it was to be *Matthew 24, Mark 13,* and *Luke 21*—what could be quicker or easier?

The next free afternoon at home, probably on a Saturday, I set about. I got out two Bibles and laid them side-by-side on the table. I opened one to *Matthew 24* and the other to *Luke 21*, where two of the accounts of Jesus' Olivet Discourse, His "Little Apocalypse," are found, and began to read them one word at a time in each account, tracing each word in each Bible with each of my two index fingers.

I can't remember why I approached the study in such a deliberate manner. I may have been afraid and didn't want to see what awful thing might lie ahead just around the next corner. I decided to take one step at a time, very slowly, with my eyes wide open, not looking for trouble and hoping not to find any. I'm certain that this kind of trepidation is common among those who are weak in their faith.

I don't know why I chose *Matthew* and *Luke* to compare, rather than *Mark.* Maybe I had a hidden aversion to *Mark* because of the doubt sown in my mind by some modern critics.

I don't even know why I wasn't just reading *Matthew.* I don't even know why I was even comparing the texts. After all, I was brought up believing strongly in the harmony of the Gospels, indeed in the harmony of the whole Word of God, including the Old and the New Testaments. This doctrine meant in essence that there were no contradictions in the Word of God. Why wouldn't just the reading of the first and most complete historical Gospel be sufficient? It had almost always been sufficient for me, although *Luke* often had special attractions. Why look for trouble? **Why was I doing this?**

I do know why I was comparing just two of the synoptic accounts and not all three at the same time. It was a matter of mental and physical limitations. I couldn't hold that much in my mind at one time and I only had two index fingers. Besides, it only requires two to compare. I'd deal with *Mark* later.

For reasons that I now find incomprehensible, for reasons that are known but to God, I proceeded in this fashion, reading *Matthew 24* and *Luke 21,* side-by-side, verse-by-verse. I was tracing and reading, tracing and reading, one word at a time…when it happened!

I had already made it past the differences in the Apostles' questions for Jesus in the two accounts without stumbling or falling from faith…*much.*

However, let me confess to you right now, that even these small differences often caused uneasiness within my heart, which was so basically set on the Bible being the infallible, inerrant, God-Breathed, verbally inspired Word of God. These were the kind of verses that my eyes actually tried to avoid and my mind strove to forget as soon as possible.

They bothered me in much the same way that the picture of the rampant grizzly bear in my first storybook did when I was a very small child. That picture so frightened me that I marked it out with a big black crayola because I was never successful in just skipping that page. I always turned that very page over and fell into that very scary trap.

My fingers were already in both records of the signs that Jesus gave his Disciples in answer to their questions about what signs would precede the destruction of Jerusalem, the End of the Age and of His Return. Luke seemed to have one more sign than Matthew, but still *this was small stuff.* In my liberal mind, basic harmony was still intact. I made it successfully all the way to *Matthew, verse 9*, and *Luke, verse 12*—but then it happened, there it was!

In an instant, harmony was **What I feared most happened!** *crushed, faith sent reeling, even the stability of my very being questioned. All in a flash.*

There, these two verses and all that followed lay side by side as they had for almost two thousand years, quietly sleeping, waiting.

Waiting to spring up and destroy the meandering, wandering fool who would in blindness and ignorance stumble upon them and be destroyed.

Backing up a couple of verses to catch the context, here is what my left index finger traced and my eyes beheld in *Matthew, verse 24:9…*

Without warning, my eyes fell upon the great *rampant grizzly*, the hidden snare, the trap, a great hidden mountain of stumbling blocks of absolutely irreconcilable verses lying jumbled across the path.

> 7   *For nation shall rise against nation, and kingdom against kingdom: and there shall be famines, and pestilences, and earthquakes, in diverse places.*
>
> 8   *All these are the beginning of sorrows.*
>
> 9   ***Then**, shall they deliver you up to be afflicted, and shall kill you: And ye shall be hated of all nations for my name's sake.*

Again, backing up a couple of verses for context, here is what my right index finger traced and what my startled mind and eyes beheld in *Luke, verse 21:12…*

> 10   *Then said he unto them, nation shall rise against nation, and kingdom against kingdom:*
>
> 11   *And great earthquakes shall be in diverse places, and famines, and pestilences; and fearful sights and great signs shall there be from heaven.*
>
> 12   ***But before all these**, they shall lay their hands on you, and persecute you, delivering you up to the synagogues, and into prisons, being brought before kings and rulers for my name's sake.*

Jolting my mind, riveting my attention, and almost stopping my heart, were the two words that set the order of these dreadful signs and even more dreadful events that they were supposed to herald in these two very different accounts. They were the word 'then' of Matthew's verse 9, and the word 'before' of Luke's verse 12. Is Matthew saying that the heralding signs come before the dreadful events that they are sent to herald? And is Luke really saying, "No Matthew, you have got it all wrong? These events must come first and then the heralding signs can appear. *What!!* What a dispute! What a conflict!

What a contradiction! I shook my head to clear my mind of cobwebs. I could not believe it. I could not even look at it again. This was a charging, rampant, raging grizzly. This was more than I could take. I got up and walked around the table shaking my head all of the way, and then slowly forced my eyes back to those fatal words again. They had not changed. Neither my mind nor my eyes had betrayed me, although I wished they had.

There must be something wrong with the translations. I raced through the house, pulling translation after translation from the shelves, all English, of course. To

These words of absolute contradiction *were there*.

my growing dismay and deepening consternation, none of them varied so much as one letter from that which first confronted and confounded me. Later, review of the English/Greek interlinear texts and Greek lexicons and consultation with real Greek scholars confirmed this solid witness to the faithful constancy of these English translations in these two opposing verses.

I sat back, mind racing. What can this possibly mean? I am not dreaming. I am not hallucinating. The Lord's words in English are simple enough. As a matter of fact, they can't get simpler. The sentence structures are simple. We are not dealing with parable or elliptical speech or allegories or figures of speech or anything that reeks of theological hyperbole or even of theological depth.

Yet *Matthew* and *Luke* have *Jesus* giving exactly the opposite order of the very same, very important set of events. They have *Him bluntly* and *plainly contradicting Himself*, if you would believe them both. These two records of *His sayings* stand diametrically opposed. They *contradict* each other. They couldn't be any more opposite if one said *yes* and the other said *no*; or if one said *day* and the other said *night*, or if one said *before* and the other said *after*.

In fact, that is exactly what they said in the frighteningly contradictory verses of *Luke 21:12* and *Matthew 24:9* where my fingers, mind and heart stopped.

After all, I believed that these two records were supposed to be telling the same story. I had never even entertained the thought that this was not the case. The weight of 1700 years of teachings and traditions that this was indeed the case, unconsciously pressing down on me, *had become my belief.* The results were my unbounded astonishment and consternation and even disbelief at the *Word of God*, which I had just read that *contradicted* my belief!

But *Luke*, in *verse 12*, clearly records that Jesus had said, "But *before* all these things," meaning that *before* the signs of the End that *Luke* had just recorded in *verses 10* and *11* could take place, some other terrible things would have to happen *first*, including the *Destruction of Jerusalem!*

In total contradiction, *Matthew* in *verse 9* records that Jesus had said "*then*," meaning this very same long, detailed series of terrible things, including the Destruction of Jerusalem *would take place after the Signs of the End.*

Tell me, does this long detailed series of terrible events take place before (according to *Luke*) or after (according to *Matthew*) the Signs of the End? Which is it? It can't be both.

To heighten anxiety, both records of this long detailed series of terrible events in *Matthew* and *Luke* included a description

Which of these guys got it right? Which got it wrong?

of the Destruction of Jerusalem, with the same route of escape prescribed in each case, "Flee to the mountains of Judea." This is exactly what His disciples had asked about. This is what had so agitated their minds in the first place.

Question of the Hour, Question of the Ages! Will the Destruction of Jerusalem come *before* or *after* the signs that the disciples had just asked for and that Jesus had just given them? Before or after?

In the following years, which Gospel account should they trust for their escape?

My roiling mind and confused and anguished heart cried out, "Tell me plainly, if You are indeed the Messiah, and the Bible is a true and trustworthy record of *Your life, Your works,* and especially, *Your words.* Tell me plainly, do the signs come first and then the Dreaded Events they foretell, or somehow do the dreaded events come before the signs, which seems to make no sense at all. Why am I being confused?

Are *You* really just an uncertain prophet as the world has always said, talking out of both sides of *Your mouth,* covering all bases? Please God, don't strike me dead for such blasphemous thoughts flying through my head. And why have I just now seen these verses? Where have I been? After all, these time-sequencing words, *before* and *then,* are not dealing with some trivial side issue. They are at the very heart of the matter that *You* have just been asked about by Your *other* bewildered disciples. The fixed and certain help *Your* disciples had desperately asked for, has instead become a bewildering confused riddle—not a comforting answer and sure guide.

In Your answers You are dealing with the fundamental issue of the question of signs and times that Your disciples had just asked You about.

And of huge additional significance, Your answers are also fundamental to the structure of what You are declaring to be the definitive history of mankind from that day until the end of the age, all told before hand.

Your total validity and reputation as a prophet, yes, even Your *Messiah-ship* rest upon the accuracy of *Your* answer until the end of time. Can You be trusted as the *Incarnation of the Holy Omniscient God,* as very Deity, who knows the end from the beginning or are *You* just guessing like everybody else? The answer to this question makes all of the difference in the world.

As these two contradicting verses stand, they make the meaning of these two whole chapters containing Your Great Discourse on coming events, especially Your Return and the End Of The Age Worse than useless.

It makes them *chaos and confusion.*

It would have been far better for us if these chapters just weren't in the *Bible* at all, if they had just never been written. It would have been far better for us if some godly ancient Christian father had just been wise and powerful enough to have challenged them at some ancient council and had them removed from our knowledge by majority vote or back room negotiations. It would have been far better for us if they had just edited them out of writ, sight, memory and history.

In their desperate need, fear and confusion Your disciples had asked You for help. Did You give them, deliberate confusion, instead of light? Asking for a drink of water and a loaf of bread, did You give them poison and a scorpion? Was the Almighty, through You, just toying with them? What kind of game is this, anyway? Is this the way the Father treats His children? Is this a foretaste of what we are to expect at Your hands from here on out to the end of time?

What is at stake in these verses is not just the trustworthiness of the Scriptures, but also, the validity of any claim that You might make that YOU are the Messiah, the only One who like the Father, could tell the end from the beginning. Indeed, Your very claim to be One with Father, very Deity, is in question here. Very heavy stuff indeed! Woe is me. Woe is us.

And at least as vexing to me, at the hideous moment of the grizzly discovery, was the fact that the dark cloud of these contradictions obscured not only the heart of the very question that so troubled Your hearers then, but also the heart of the questions that so concern this very present generation.

After all, it was to determine the truth of these contentious matters that lead me to study YOUR simple "Little Apocalypse" in the first place. Was my quest to be so ignominiously ended and so very quickly? What I feared most had fallen upon me.

These are not subtle differences to be set aside and dealt with later, if ever. These are fundamental opposites, screaming out their challenges at the highest level. Together they constitute a fatal flaw to the literalist. They are massive roadblocks and barricades. They block the way.

They scream out their defiance. You shall not pass here and retain your integrity, your sanity and your faith. At least one of the three will have to go!

Can I walk with Him any further? But where shall I go? To whom shall I turn? In whom and what shall I trust?

The emotions and thoughts that racked my brain and flooded my soul were a raging torrent.

Dear reader, please allow me to interrupt my tale of dread and woe at this point to bring to you what could be some life sustaining cautionary notes before proceeding.

First, please don't abandon this tale or the reading of *Matthew 24* and *Luke 21* until you have read the rest of this fearful story. It has a turning point.

However, if you finish the rest of my story, don't ever forget its beginning, its origin, its basis, which is the eye popping, mind jolting and heart stopping, challenge of Luke 21:12. For this verse is not only the beginning, it is the heart of this story. But far more importantly, it is The heart of two of the most important stories of this age for our lives

The first story is the trustworthy telling of the true history of the world by Jesus from the time He spoke these words until this day and even to the end of the age. With *Luke 21:12* locked in your brain and seared on your heart, the foreknowledge of this history is now, perhaps for the first time, available to you. Even the End of this Age can now be clearly discerned by you, even if you are also just a simple wayfaring fool. *Read this story in Part II, The View From The Mountain.*

The second story is of the age-old cover-up instituted to hide the truth and the impact of what Jesus really said on the Mount of Olives about the history of the world and the End of the Age. This cover-up, instituted early, continues to this very day. The story is also about the dire consequences of the great cover up, especially for this generation. Read this story in *Part III, But Before All These Things,* for insight, both for encouragement and for warning. Read it for your very life and for your very own personal escape.

In attempting to deliver a clear and concise account of these two stories much detail has necessarily been left out. *You must find it for yourself.* The detail that has been supplied is often presented in a truncated form. Tables have been used, as well as abbreviations, footnotes and references, all intended to clarify, but often interrupting the flow of narrative. If you get lost or lose interest, God forbid, treat the tables as an appendix to be studied later and move on. But mark them for later prayer and study for there is a wealth of understanding to be gleaned from them, if you are willing.

But of foremost importance, remember *Luke 21:12. It is the Word of God.* Although it may have been hidden from you; it is now yours, your treasure and *your responsibility.* The story that it can now reveal to you is one more sure foundation for your hope, reserved for you by our Father in and for these last days.

He has, indeed, come with us to the end of the age, just as *He promised.*

Am I saying that these stories are as vital as the good news that God so loved the world that He gave His only begotten

Son that whosoever believes on Him should not perish but inherit Eternal Life?

No, I am not.

The importance of these stories lies in the fact that they go a long way in explaining why so many souls of so many generations, including especially this last one, have either not heard or understood this good news, and why the believers of this generation do not recognize this, *the season of His return.* These stories are vital to this last generation, for preparing, equipping and sustaining the Saints for *the final battle of their faith.*

Jesus tried to rip the blinders off of the eyes of that final generation under the law in His day, in order for some of them to see and to understand what God really had in store for them. He is doing it again today with the *fulfillment of prophecy* for those who have eyes to see and ears to hear in this final generation.

Before bringing these cautionary notes to you, I was relating the state of my mind at the moment of the hideous discovery. The emotions and thoughts that racked my brain and flooded my soul were a raging torrent. Blasphemy was in my heart and on my lips, but then....

Then slowly blasphemy was condemned and shamed. Raging emotions and thoughts dropped to a more deliberate pace. Finally, at last, they came to a peaceful rest. First, there had been the shock, then the fright and recoiling rebellion, now came faith, repentance, contemplation and the slowly growing determination to get to the bottom of this very peculiar matter, if God would permit. I would not lose my faith. The *Lord of Heaven and Earth* had never failed me. He was trustworthy. I would trust Him now. What else could I do?

In this heart and mind of faithful resignation I began a very slow and very deliberate prayer to our God,

"These are Your words, O God. I have trusted You and Your words lo these many years and You have never failed me or given me reason to question You, or doubt Your word, although many times I have not understood You. I have often been slothful. I have often failed You. I have not always obeyed. I have often sinned. I am sorry and I repent. Right now I haven't a clue about what is going on, or what You are trying to tell me, but I believe You. I trust You. Where possible I even want to understand You or at least to understand what You want me to understand. You have spoken plainly and I don't get it. My arrogant spirit of knowledge and understanding is broken. I know the problem is my fault. It is not Your fault. You are blameless. I hold You blameless in my own heart. I no longer accuse You. Forgive me. I know You do. I know You have. My heart is at peace. Your will be done. Now in peace guide me carefully through Your word. I know that in Your own good time You will show me Your will when and if it is Your will for me to understand. My heart is at peace. I will wait on You, O my God."

In this brokenness, the raging torrent became still waters.

And so, armed with brokenness and faith and with peace in my heart, I read on, confident that He would in *His own good time* and in *His own good way* make all things clear according to *His own good will*.

And that He has begun.

In this particular matter, He has let me slip the ancient and powerful bonds of slavery to the traditions of men and set me free to walk in the light of *His Word*. I have begun this walk as one awaking from sleep.

And this is what I want to share with you, if you will let me. If you will let Him.

What for me was at first, the frightening surprise, the great anomaly of the Gospels, or at least, the great anomaly of the Olivet Discourse, has, in the course of time, become instead, a very clear, orderly and straightforward account of Jesus' own telling of the entire future from that day in which He spoke until that day in which He returns. And this clear foretelling of the future and its clear and totally accurate fulfillment in history to date has become for me *the surest, steadiest, sign that He is indeed the promised Messiah and that God is not only still active in this world's affairs, but He is on schedule and it is time to get ready.*

> He has come with us to the *End of the Age.*

My earlier erroneous perception that there was a fatal Gospel Anomaly was slowly replaced by the realization that there was *no anomaly in the Scriptures at all*, but rather, astoundingly, that there has been for lo, these many years, *a great anomaly in church thought and teaching, and consequently and very unfortunately also in church and world history.*

You see Jesus was right all along in both accounts. Matthew got it right. Luke got it right. The Holy Spirit got it right! Luke and Matthew *only appear* to contradict each other *only* if you *presuppose* they are telling the very same story. And that has been the erroneous presupposition of the church these many centuries. *What is manifestly obvious from the text is that they are not both telling the very same short story at all and they both got it right.* Luke is telling the very first part of a very long story and Matthew is telling the very last part of this very same, very long story. That is what the Scriptures plainly say.

So much for seventeen hundred years of tradition.

What at first to me was a great mystery in the plain *Word of God* was resolved for me by *God, Himself, through His Spirit and through His Word.* My initial great concern for the consistency of *His Word* was soon replaced by a deep pondering of that great dark gash in world history, *the great censorship*, the great deception that has been at work along these lines at least since man expounded these *Scriptures* in the fourth century.

An astounding part of this mystery of iniquity is how could Satan have possibly obscured *foundational truth*, so plainly written, for so long, from so many, to result in such a devastating history of consequences, that is, even now, in our own day, reaching its horrible crescendo.

Obviously, part of the adversary's strategy was to simply hide the verses in the *Olivet Discourse* that make the true story so simple and so easy to understand. He hid them in plain sight by the use of the "Harmony of the Gospels" stratagem. Through his emissaries he had led us to believe that the stories told in *Luke* and *Matthew* were just two accounts of the very same events and so most of us *never looked* to see for ourselves if this were true or not.

That is why I was so startled to see this age-old tradition, planted in my heart as unquestioned truth by generations, even centuries, of orthodoxy so violently challenged by the simple *Words of the Scriptures*. It took some time for my eyes and heart to adjust to the light. In the mean time I was completely confused, not willing to let go what I believed to be true, initially even charging *God* with incompetence at the very least.

> My, my, the power of tradition to even cause us to blaspheme and question *God!*

Is this how Satan was able to manipulate the religious crowd so easily to crucify our Lord in His day?

If *the Scriptures* really meant what they so plainly said, my whole view of the Christian faith would have to be radically revised including significant elements of *Jesus' purpose, plan, kingdom, world history, future events and what I am supposed to be doing now.*

I do not yet know the full impact on my life of this encounter with the Word of God.

This harmony of the Gospel blind-fold strategy certainly worked well against me, but I am neither a scholar nor, unfortunately, even a simple honest man of faith. Is it possible that all of the faithful and learned teachers in the history of the church have been as easily fooled? Or, maybe there is a broader, deeper, more sinister multi-century conspiracy at work than the simple, but so effective, exploitation of indifference, sin, sloth and ignorance that so entrapped me? Or does it really make any difference whether there is or not? After all, Satan is behind all sin and is the father of all of the lies that almost always must precede sin in order for sin to entrap us.

Or is this simply, in this very late present hour, the time that God has chosen, in the closing days of this era, to make these things clear to His Gentile people; just as He promised in *Daniel 12:10* to reveal the mysteries of the timing of the end, to His Jewish people as the end draws near?

Now having the facts as Jesus so plainly presented them, a haunting question rose in my heart, a haunting question with very dark and foreboding edges. Why?

With such a consistent pattern of deception in place for such an extended period of time, the indelible mark of conspiracy was, and is, written all over the face of this intrigue, but why?

Such a long-legged conspiracy must have purposes, fixed and steady goals to be accomplished. What were those goals? Why was this conspiracy commissioned? Who is its patron?

I searched to discover *the effects* of these simple, but stupendous, misunderstandings, mistakes, oversights and maybe even purposeful slights of hand or tongue, believing that in *the effects* I would find the *why* and the *who*. I would find the *motive* and the *culprit*. It didn't take long, or much insight, to come up with a gut-wrenching list of the effects of this conspiracy to silence The Word of God in These Scriptures. Although there are a multitude of reasons for hiding this verse, and its many companion verses, the heavies that lead the list of damnation are:

- To discredit *Jesus as Prophet and Son of God* in the eyes of most of the world for most centuries. After all, He claimed to tell the future and He couldn't even get the story straight; *and it worked.*
- To discredit the *Word of God* as truth, as a reliable message from the Father to His children for their instruction, guidance and salvation; *and it worked.*
- To hide the *God ordained* and *God foretold* course of history from many generations; *and it worked.*
- To re-enslave the people who had just been set free by God to serve the *Prince of Peace* who had said that *His Kingdom* was not of this world, else *His servants* would fight; to re-

enslave them to serve the kings of this earth again in their pursuit of worldly power; and it worked.

- To extinguish the rights of the *Jewish nation* to the promises that God made to them and, as if it were possible, to extinguish the *Jews* themselves; *and it almost worked.*
- And to blind this final generation to the rapidly approaching time of its decision either to be delivered or to stay behind; *and it is working.*

And now, let's get to the bottom of this matter by telling the two most important stories of this age and of your life, right next to the Gospel.

If you are willing, you can read and understand the first great story of this day and of your life in the following *Part II, The View from the Mountain, The True History of the World as Foretold by Jesus on the Mount of Olives*. This *Part II* will lead you, if you are ready and willing, through the mystery of The Astounding Anomaly of the Gospels to the clear light of day of what *Jesus* really said about the future and its immediate impact on us.

If you really want to understand the true basis of world history to this present day and really want to know what is going to happen next, read this.

With *faith*, *brokenness*, *prayer* and *meditation* on your part, *He* will make it all clear to you, too.

If you are willing, you can read and understand the second great story of this day and of your life in *Part III, But Before All These Things*. This story is an attempt at partially unveiling the mystery of iniquity that has wrought such havoc on the church and on the world in every century by hiding the truth of this phrase and its companions. This mystery is even now, forging its final diabolical explosion of chaos.

This final Part III is a warning to the children of God, that the adversary's long, and effective campaign is now coming to a close and that the ultimate test of faith is almost in sight for everyone in the whole world. Be on your alert. Get ready. He is at the door.

Not only is God still active in the affairs of men and nations today, and always has been, but Satan is still at work as well. Satan is the author of the conspiracy.

The raging spiritual battle of the ages in heaven and on earth of which we have often been so oblivious is reaching its climax and soon no man of the slightest spiritual discernment can be oblivious to it any longer.

This is no dream. It appears to be beginning now. You will most likely see it all yourself.

The View from the Mountain

*The True History of the World
As Foretold by Jesus on
The Mount of Olives*

The Story As He Told It

Now here is the story that Jesus told on the Mount of Olives. Read it slowly and thoughtfully and you will understand exactly what Jesus said. Read all of The View From The Mountain and you will also have a better understanding of exactly what He meant. What He said is incontrovertible and exceedingly clear. What He said is also what He meant. And it is also easy to understand.

I was wrong. I was terribly wrong in thinking that God had really let us down by making a muddle out of the Record of the Olivet Discourse. God was right and did it right, as He always does. He is also so wonderfully patient and long-suffering with those of us caught in Satan's web of trusting man and his traditions. But His patience has its limits and He is not slack as some men count slackness, but will call us all into account. I also marvel at how abysmally ignorant I was (and still am) of the extent of the huge power of Satan over men when the *Holy Spirit* is grieved or quenched in them or totally absent from their hearts.

Nearly two thousand years ago, on the Mount of Olives, Jesus gave astounding answers to some very fearful questions asked Him by His disciples. In the process of answering their questions He told them about the future that they and the whole world would face. From that very day to this very day —and even to the end of the age.

A vital notice to this doubting generation

The really over arching significance of a man sitting on the Mount of Olives two thousand years ago and precisely laying out the history of the world to this very day is that the man could not have been only a man. This is why Satan has striven so mightily to conceal the facts of this *Revelation* by Jesus by trying so desperately to muddle our understanding of His teachings from the Mount of Olives. If the world understood that Jesus clearly told the very end of this age from it's beginning, they might believe that He and the Father are One just as He claimed. Muddle the prophecy and no one can see its fulfillment and Satan's mission is accomplished. That is exactly what the church has done so effectively for so long and is one of the main reasons that the world at large has not believed and does not now believe that *Jesus is the Messiah.*

But make this prophecy by Jesus clear, and the consequent exact fulfillment of it in history can establish Him in the eyes of the sincere and honest seeker not just as a true prophet of God but actually as the everlasting I am, the only one who knows the end from the beginning. Then they can understand who He really is because Jesus is the only one who has ever lived who has done that thing that God said that He alone could do. You see, God makes the following unique, claim for Himself in *Isaiah 46:9–10*:

"For I am God, and there is none else; I am God, And there is none like Me; declaring the end from the beginning, and from ancient times things that are not yet done"—

And Jesus did just that! He declared the *end* from the *beginning*!

What Jesus actually said on that day on the Mount of Olives, declaring the end from the beginning, has come to pass, clearly and in order! He is, therefore, Lord and God. No other man, god man, seer or prophet living today or in any age of the past has done this; not even God's own prophets were ever given full understanding of what they saw, and certainly not Mary Baker Eddy, Edgar Casey, not that Frenchman whose name I can't remember, not Joe Smith, and not Mohammed. Jesus is who He claimed to be, Lord and God.

Isn't it amazing and wonderful that fulfilled **Isn't it amazing and** prophecy, the final incontrovertible, objective **wonderful?** proof of Jesus as His Son, indeed as His Very Self, would have its heaviest impact fall upon This Generation?

This generation, which is now in the process of seeing it all fulfilled;

This generation, which is the furthest removed from the faith-sustaining miracles of His life;

This generation, which is filled with a thousand competing gods, demigods and non gods and their frenetic clamoring adherents and false prophets;

This generation, which is dominated by cynics, scoffers and those who are asleep in and out of the church;

This generation, which will desperately need all the support for its faith that Heaven can supply, as all earthly and visible supports crumble around us and come crashing down;

This generation, of which Jesus asked, "Will there be faith on earth when the Son of Man returns?"

Isn't it amazing and wonderful? "For the testimony of Jesus is the Spirit of Prophecy." Praise God. No wonder Satan hates prophecy! It proves that Jesus is Lord and God.

Yes, the Son, as He promised, has not left us **The Testimony of Jesus** without a comforter and witness, but has, in fact, **is the Spirit of Prophecy.** come with us, even to the end of the age, just as He promised that He would with a great testimony: prophecy fulfilled before our very eyes!

We can depend on the very few yet-unfulfilled elements of Jesus' prophecy from the Mount of Olives coming to pass, on time and in order, because He is God who declares the end from the beginning as the last two thousand years of precisely fulfilled prophecy have proved.

Read on and let the record speak for itself and to your heart.

"And so we have the prophetic word confirmed, which you do well to heed as a light that shines in a dark place, until the day

dawns and the morning star rises in your hearts." (Jesus is the morning star) "Worship God! for the testimony of Jesus is the Spirit of Prophecy." (2Peter1:19 and Revelations 19:10)

The questions that He answered that day on the *Mount of Olives* so long ago came tumbling from the lips of men who were seized by great fear. They were alarmed and apprehensive, fearfully stirred by the terrible and foreboding words that Jesus had just spoken while walking on the Temple Mount. They had been with Him on this, His last walk through the *Holy Precincts* that He called His Father's House. He would not walk there again. They heard the last words of warning Jesus would speak to His beloved Jerusalem and to His beloved people before they seized Him and executed Him, playing the roles assigned to them by the one who vainly sought to destroy Him.

These words which He spoke that day contained a fearful prophecy, for Jesus declared before them all.

"As for these things which you behold, the days will come, in which there shall not be left one stone upon another, that will not be thrown down".

His enemies were just waiting for such words as these against the Holy Place. To their twisted hearts they were clearly blasphemy. They were used against Him in His trial. They were twisted, either misunderstood or not believed, back then with dire results for those who either misunderstood or who did not believe them. They still go, twisted, misunderstood or not believed even to this day, posing equally dreadful consequences to come for those who, in like manner, still so abuse them.

This prophecy of His on that day was the culmination of a flood of wild and foreboding things that Jesus had been declaring. For a taste of what they feared and why they were anxious, read the record of what He had been telling them in *Luke 11:29–52, 17:22–37; 18:7–8* and in *Matthew 23:32–39*.

These terrible pronouncements of His culminated in the following dreadfully damning and imminently prophetic convicting and sentencing of His people, His Jerusalem and His generation.

"Fill up then the measure of the guilt of your fathers. You serpents, you brood of vipers how shall you escape the sentence of hell? Therefore behold, I am sending you prophets and wise men and scribes. Some of them you will kill and crucify, and some of them you will scourge in your synagogues and persecute from city to city, that upon you shall fall the guilt of all the righteous blood shed on earth from the blood of righteous Abel to the blood of Zechariah, the son of Berechiah, whom you murdered between the temple and the altar. Truly I say to you, all these things shall come upon this generation. O Jerusalem, Jerusalem, who kills the prophets and stones those who are sent to her. How often I wanted to gather your children together the way a hen gathers her chicks under her wings, and you were unwilling. Behold your house is being left to you desolate! For I say unto you from now on you shall not see me until you say, "Blessed is He who comes in the Name of the Lord!" Matthew 23:32–39.

> Truly I say to **you,** all these things **shall** come upon this generation.

And within 38 years of the day He spoke this prophecy, on the ninth of AV (In our month and year of August 70 AD) they saw it. What He prophesied came to pass, when, where and how He said it would. Look back to that prophecy and its fulfillment, to judge His authority for all time and to calibrate His accuracy for us today

> Jesus had said that fearful retribution would be demanded of Jerusalem in your own lifetime. You shall see it in your generation.

On the Mount of Olives, where they followed Jesus after His dreadful proclamation that the stones would be thrown down, *Peter, James, John* and *Andrew* privately took Jesus aside and asked Him, undoubtedly, with great anxiety and urgency when this terrifying thing would happen and what would be the signs of the approach of this devastation of the Temple and desolation of Jerusalem. In light of His earlier teachings they also asked Him what would be the signs of His Return and of the End of the Age.

His answers were of utmost interest to those who heard Him then, since He had already told them that they would experience the desolation of Jerusalem in their very own lifetime, in their generation. If they believed Him, they were undoubtedly frightened. They certainly wanted to be prepared to escape or cope, if at all possible. They wanted to know when it would happen, what warning signs they should look for and what they could possibly do to escape.

In compassion He answered them directly and abundantly, telling them not only about the dreadful happenings that would befall them in their own generation, but telling them the entire future history of their race. He gave them, in detail, three separate sets of warning signs and escape routes from two distinctly different catastrophes, which would befall Jerusalem approximately two thousand years apart! I hope you will be convinced of this after you have finished studying the record in *Luke 21:12–24, Matthew 24:9–28* and in *Josephus*.

Some thirty-eight years after He gave them the answers to their questions, the first part of the first series of events, which He foretold precisely and in some detail, came to its horrific end exactly as He prophesied. The answers that Jesus had given them served as a calendar and a foundation for their hope in the intervening years and as an exact guide for the preservation of their lives for that first generation of believers. The prophecy also gave them (and us) the warning signs of the approach of the final disaster and His instructions for the escape of the last generation of believers, most likely our very own selves.

Read on, I think you will agree.

The exact fulfillment of Jesus' prophecy leading up to and including the destruction of Jerusalem in 70 AD and the events that followed is the perfect proof test of the accuracy of all of the rest of what He had to say. He said it was going to happen and when; and it happened and on schedule! In the run up to 70 AD God left us a template of what is to come. If you want proof of the accuracy of what Jesus says about the events yet to come, if you want a template, look back at 70 AD.

Now, nearly two thousand years after Jesus answered their questions, the last part of the first series of events that He foretold has been accomplished just as He said it would be and the second series of events that He foretold appears to have begun. The words of His prophecy will again, in the same manner, preserve the true believers of the final generation by again providing the warning signs and His instructions for escape. Trusting Jesus' answers to His disciples' questions will save the believers of the final generation from the destruction to come, just as it saved the first generation of believers in 70 AD.

What He said *would happen* and *when, did happen* and then, what He says is *going to happen* and *when, will happen* and then–

Four *apostles*, according to *Mark*, privately heard Jesus' answers. The answers are preserved for us in three gospel accounts. Jesus' answers were in plain language, plainly spoken. He laid out the future of Jerusalem in important detail from that time until the end of the age. His answers were bluntly prophetic. They were also: plain, clear, without figure of speech or symbolism. Straight information was delivered in a straightforward manner without mystery and requires only faith in Him and His word to be understood today.

Prelude to the rest of the story

In spite of Jesus' unquestionable intention to be understood and in spite of the clarity with which He presented the matter, the adversary, Satan, has very successfully slipped in and scrambled this prophecy in the minds of most people to this very day. To discover the truth of what Jesus actually said, it is only necessary to read the words, which He spoke. But to understand, one must clear the mind of all preconceptions gathered from whatever sources, especially those usually unreliable sources from which we get most of our information and simply to pay very careful attention to *The Scriptures*, which the *Holy Spirit* has faithfully delivered to us. But this simple task turns out to be one of the hardest tasks that we in our flesh will ever undertake. Yes, to understand what Jesus said is both easy and simple.

But to discard our *culture*, that all-pervasive milieu that engulfs our every thought and determines all of our values is very difficult. How does a fish know that it is wet? How do we hear or see or know beyond what every voice that we ever trusted has ever told us? The *traditions of our society* whether based on the *Word of God* or based on *our traditions* which we think are based on the *Word of God* guide our steps and provide the answers to all the questions we've ever thought of or had the courage to ask.

It is extremely hard to break out of the mold of tradition whether you are a *Christian, Jew, Hindu, Muslim* or whatever. Tradition is almost always the greatest challenge to our faith and its greatest test.

It was precisely the failure of the Jewish leaders of Jesus' day to critically reexamine the accepted orthodoxy of their day, that is, their traditions, in the light of His words that caused them to totally miss the day of their visitation.

Very learned and wise fathers from ancient times had studied the coming of the Messiah very closely, using all the skill and reason that they possessed to discover the time and manner of His first advent and somehow they had missed it. Most of the people in His day who got it right had no confidence in their own righteousness or wisdom. A lot of the people who missed it had overweening confidence in their wisdom, knowledge and righteousness. Interesting isn't it? And very instructive.

Long before the time of His arrival the wise men's errors, which may seem minor and of no consequence had been slowly transformed into unquestioned orthodoxy by succeeding generations. What may have first been set forth as a theory subject to debate became, in time, undisputed facts by this thoughtless process. These seemingly minor errors obtained sanctity simply because they were old and had been accepted by the fathers. So when the Messiah did arrive that generation which should have been ready to receive Him missed Him.

The leaders and the people of the day of His first coming missed Him although they were face to face with what would appear to be the overwhelming evidence of: *The prophecies concerning Him*; *The signs and miracles that He performed*, and even *His Resurrection*. They set aside the *Word of God*. Instead, teaching and believing the traditions and doctrines of men, they and their followers *perished*.

What a testimony the sad failure of that generation is to the tyranny over man of the almost supreme power of unquestioned tradition and blind submission to orthodoxy! How ancient and powerful indeed is peer pressure

The trap of *tradition* awaits every citizen of the world today as it has for every generation. It has been said that God has no grandchildren. In every generation, He has only sons and daughters born to Him through the water and the Spirit, each one of whom must individually come to Him through their faith in Him, *not in their father's faith, and not through their faith in their father's faith. Unquestioned tradition and orthodoxy are traps of Satan.* You cannot inherit eternal life from your family, your tribe or your religion; it

A seeking heart that listens to *God* is absolutely necessary to life in the Spirit. We are indeed made in *God's image* and He demands that each one of us, as one of *His children*, take responsibility for our own heart and entrust it to Him alone and to *no one else.*

is a gift directly from God to you. You must trade your faith in what has been handed down from the traditions of your fathers for the pure and undiluted truth of what He has said.

In that, and that alone, can you trust.

This requires of every person of every generation the fundamental decision of life: This world or Him.

He is a jealous God. We are to have none before Him.

He summed up His condemnation of the hand-me-down faith of family, family values and family allegiances when He said, "If you don't love Me more than *Mother* or *Father*, you can have no part of Me."

The persistent power of tribal religions and man's preference for them rather than for God is proved beyond a shadow of doubt to any objective observer by the devotion in this day of the hundreds of millions of followers of *Buddha*, the *Hindu gods*, the *Shinto faith*, *African Animism*, *Mohammed*, *atheism*, and thousands of brands of *Christianity*.

Mankind has almost always universally preferred the comfort of man's company and agreement to that of God, and this is ever so more true today.

He is a jealous God. We are to have none before Him

He said, "This is my beloved Son, hear ye Him".

Bluntly, be warned that the story you are about to read is far different from the *Orthodox tradition* that the *historical church* has taught and what most church people have believed for about the last seventeen hundred years (However, in the beginning of the church it was not so taught or believed). Therefore, if the story appears to be difficult to understand and its consequences appear to be inconsequential and hardly worth the effort to understand them, then let that be warning enough that the adversary has been very successful in clouding hearts and minds to these issues of vital importance. But with prayers and fresh minds and eager hearts it will be plain that the story that Jesus told is easy to understand, and the consequences of the truth that He reveals are of vital and urgent importance to those who live today.

Do not seek the faith of your fathers, nor of your youth. Instead seek the *Truth of God* from the *Word* who is *God*.

Read the next few paragraphs carefully. Hear the argument out. Trace the Scriptures in the two chapters in *Matthew* and *Luke* carefully, using the side-by-side Scriptures provided for you or your own Bible. See if the things set forth here are true or not. In several instances assertions are made before the evidence of their truth is presented. Be patient, read on, and see if these things are true or not. It will be worth your time. But first check your preconceptions at the door. This is the price of admission

Now here is the rest of the story

In *Matthew Ch. 24* and *Luke Ch. 21*, contrary to what has generally been taught these last seventeen hundred years, Jesus projects in His answer to His disciples questions, a clear time line of God's signs and the events that they portend from His day until the end of the age. They are set forth by Him for us to understand and to heed.

In addition, as complete confirmation of the story which He told, His time line, as presented in these two Chapters, has been faithfully and precisely followed by world history ever since. In fact, only a few elements of this foretelling of world history by Jesus yet remain to be fulfilled before world history itself is completed.

But those who in ages past predigested and tamed the Scriptures for us have obscured the story. Consequently, the story

> The **Lord God** of all creation is also the **Lord God** of all history

has not been recognized and, therefore, neither have the times that Jesus spoke of been recognized. You see, you were probably taught, as I was and as most Christians are, that these two accounts in *Matthew* and *Luke* of what *Jesus* said on the Mount of Olives reflect parallel reports by these writers of the same future events. This was part and parcel of the harmony of the gospels method of interpretation from at least Saint Augustine's time.

There is no evidence that this historical parallelism of these two accounts was the teaching or the understanding of the first century church. It was a teaching that may have begun in the second century, but was certainly well established by the middle of the fourth century. Although this teaching is extra-biblical and was probably not known to the first century Church, it continued from the fourth century, even to this present day. It continues today as the orthodox and unquestioned position of the historical church.

Just one of the problems of this erroneous teaching is that it totally masks what Jesus actually said and what is, therefore, going to actually happen and has, indeed, already actually happened for centuries.

As you will plainly see, if you press on, the story that Jesus tells in these two accounts is not about the same future events, but two distinctly separate series of events. And this makes a world of difference.

You will see that the Spirit moved *Luke* to record Jesus' foretelling of the events of the first two thousand years of the ensuing history. In fact, the preponderance of the details of this first part of the history actually relate to events that took place in the very first century of this present era. In fact, they took place in the 38 years between 32 AD and 70 AD. Much of the fulfillment of His foretold events is even recorded in the *New Testament*, itself, by writers who were contemporaries of Jesus. These things happened right away, very shortly after He had prophesied them. Their precise fulfillment should stand today as the standard and the proof of the accuracy of what Jesus also said about the events that are yet to come which are mainly recorded in *Matthew's* account.

You will see that the Spirit moved *Matthew* to give us the details of the last generation of this age. In fact, most of what He details takes place in the very last years of this final generation. *Matthew 24* records almost nothing of what Jesus said about anything before our generation. Matthew's very brief history essentially begins with the five signs that initiate the final seven years of this age.

The acts of the first generation are foretold in *Luke* only.

The acts of the last generation are foretold in *Matthew* almost exclusively.

This difference in the time address of these two accounts is exactly the significance and the impact of the, *"But before all these things"* of *Luke 21:12* and the starkly contrasting *"Then"* of *Matthew 24:9* which at first so astounded me. Only by seeing, rather than ignoring, the extraordinary differences in these two verses can we understand the time line of history that Jesus delivered to us so clearly. Otherwise all is confusion.

Harmonizing the Scriptures, that is, attempting to make these two narratives relate to the same period of history as if they were parallel stories, rather than relating sequentially as two different parts of the same ongoing saga as the Scriptures plainly set them forth to be, effectively hid these differences from most scholars, teachers and commentators of most generations of this age, including this present one, with devastating results.

Many an ancient commentator (and modern as well) labored mightily to prove that the two descriptions of each pair of "matching" events in the two accounts related to the same event. However, often not a word was addressed to the patent evidence from *Luke 21:12* and *Matthew 24:9* that these two series of events lay many years apart. They weren't the same events. They would not even occur within a thousand years of each other!

The probable evil origin, and the certainly dreadful results, of this complete obfuscation of the true story by the hiding of the differences of these two verses and many other companion verses is further addressed in *Part III, But Before All These Things*.

The detailed structure of the story

Bibles please.

It is written in *Mathew 24, Mark 13* and *Luke 21* that on the Mount of Olives Jesus was asked about the future and *that Jesus told the future, all the way to the end of the age and He told it clearly.*

To most easily understand what follows and to recover the truth of what Jesus really said please consider *for the moment* that:

- The Holy Spirit selected *Jewish Matthew* to carry this message *primarily* to the believers of the *Jewish nation* of the final generation just as He had chosen Daniel, almost 600 years earlier, for the very same task.
- And that He selected *Gentile Luke* to carry this message *primarily* to the *Gentile Christians*, especially of the first and last generations.

To unravel the confusion of the ages wrought by the attempt to "harmonize" the Gospels and to recover the true story all we have to do is simply look at these two records verse by verse and take their plain language at face value. We just have to take God at His word.

To begin our recovery of the truth let us look closely at Matthew's record first. Then we will examine Luke's very different record carefully making note of the differences.

Then the truth will become self evident.

But you must be a careful student, because these Scriptures have not been taken seriously by most as a clear revelation of God's will for many centuries. You must carefully guard against a possible ingrained indifference or carelessness that you may have unconsciously inherited from your spiritual forebears. You will probably have to deprogram a very thorough job of brainwashing!

Let us get our Bibles out and see what Jesus really told us in these two records.

Matthew in relating *Jesus' prophecy of all coming history* wrote primarily to the Jewish Nation, which Paul said in Romans 11 would be partially blinded until the fullness of the Gentiles comes in, which fullness is an event very late in history and *hasn't happened yet.* Because of the Jew's blindness in the early and the intervening years as prophesied by Paul, *Matthew* skips the early and later phases of world history in his record to the Jews (They wouldn't be reading it anyway, would they?) Instead, he goes directly to the events at the close of the age when God will open their eyes by means of the chastisements of the last generation, during the time that *Jeremiah 30:7* calls the time of Jacob's trouble. This End of Age chastisement will descend on the whole world, but especially on the Jews and on Jerusalem for the very purpose of opening their eyes to their salvation. *Then they will read Matthew.* Most of them are not reading it, even yet, but their time is rapidly coming.

At that time Matthew's record will give the Jews great encouragement in their time of great tribulation. It will be the time of their purification and refinement through the fire of chastisement that is foretold in Isaiah, Jeremiah, Daniel, Zechariah, Matthew, Mark, Luke, Revelation, and many other Old and New Testament Scriptures. Then their eyes will be opened and they will say, *"Blessed is He who comes in the Name of the Lord" Matthew 23:39.* Then *"The Redeemer Will Come To Zion, And To Those Who Turn From Transgression In Jacob." Says the Lord"* in *Isaiah 59:20.* Then *"All Israel will be saved."* as Paul Prophesies in *Romans 11:26.*

In our investigation of *Matthew's 24th chapter record* of *Jesus' foretelling of the history of the world on the Mount Of Olives* let us begin by carefully looking at Jesus' Response in Verses 7 and 8 to the questions of *The Signs* that will precede *His Return*, the *End of the Age* and the *Destruction of the Temple* that were asked of Him by His disciples in Verse 3. Altogether Jesus gives six signs that foretell the beginning *and* the end of The Tribulation. But in These *two verses*, only the first five signs, which foretell only of its beginning are given. (The significance of this distinction between the first five signs and the sixth sign that foretells its end, which Matthew doesn't give until Verse 29, will become evident later in this study and especially in the study of Luke's record. Just make note of it here.)

Jesus then describes what happens *during* The Tribulation in Verses 9–28. He says that the first five signs, which are: *nation will rise against nation, kingdom against kingdom, famines, pestilences, and earthquakes in various places* not only herald this coming end of the age tribulation, but they are also, in fact, the very first phase of it. Jesus says in Verse 8 that they are its birth pains.

Now in verse 9 following the *five beginning signs*, Jesus says, *"Then they will deliver you up to tribulation and kill you and you will be hated of all nations for my name's sake."* This verse begins the detailed description of the events of the main phase of the end of age times of the greatest ever distress, The Time of Jacob's Trouble, The Tribulation which commences with these *first five signs*.

In *verses 10–14* Jesus continues to describe the dreadful events of The Tribulation, *"and then many will be offended, will betray one another and will hate one another. Then many false prophets will rise up and deceive many. And because lawlessness will abound, the love of many will grow cold. But he who endures to the end will be saved. And this Gospel of the kingdom will be preached in all the world as a witness to all the nations and then the end will come."*

This description includes events to the very end of The Tribulation, however, in the next few verses, Jesus loops back to fill in some vital details that relate to The Escape Sign that will occur in The middle of The Tribulation and the dreadful events that follow that sign in the second half of The Tribulation.

In Verse 15 Jesus gives *the escape sign* that His disciples had asked for, to enable the believers to escape Jerusalem before its desolation. *"Therefore when you see the Abomination of Desolation, spoken of by Daniel the Prophet standing in the Holy Place (whoever reads, let him understand) then let those who are in Judea flee to the mountains."*

This reference by *Jesus* to Daniel must be very important because the only *comment* on Jesus' words by the recorders that The Holy Spirit directs to be inserted in The Whole Of The Olivet Discourse is right here. Both Matthew and Mark insert it right here in their records, right in the middle of the Words of Jesus. It is: *"Whoever reads, let him understand."*

"(Whoever reads, let him understand)" A careful study of Daniel, to obtain the *understanding*, which both *Matthew and Mark urge here*, will reveal that the Abomination of Desolation standing in the Holy Place occurs in the middle of the *End Time* Tribulation. The reader will also understand that this tribulation will last seven years and the end of this tribulation will *also* be the End of the Age which the Return of Jesus will bring about. The reader will also learn that this Ending will occur three and a half years after The Abomination of Desolation is placed in the Holy Place. The reader will also understand the meaning of the sign, *The*

Abomination Of Desolation Standing in the Holy Place, because God makes it clear by means of an example.

You see, the Jews were sure that Antiochus IV Epiphanies had already fulfilled Daniel's Prophecy in 168 BC because he had. He had done so, exactly! Jesus' disciples must have really been surprised when Jesus revived this prophecy on the Mount of Olives two hundred years later and said it was yet to be fulfilled. One more time! When they finally read about the Abomination of Desolation in Matthew, The Jews will know exactly what it means and what form it will take, because they have seen it all before!

You see, Daniel had already directly addressed this very same, *very important event*, in world history *many* times in his writings and in *four* of these times he did it in almost exactly the same words as Jesus used here. Jesus does *not* readdress the *issue of the duration of The Tribulation* or *the timing of the appearance of the Abomination of Desolation* in his discourse on the Mount of Olives. *He simply makes reference to the Scriptures* where God had already abundantly addressed these issues through the prophet, Daniel, a holy man of God who also wrote as he was moved by the Holy Spirit. If you want to understand what Jesus is talking about here, you have to understand what Daniel saw in his visions from God, the main parts of which he wrote down.

Because Matthew and Mark implore that we understand this reference of Jesus to Daniel we will study it again in greater detail in the next section.

Of course, Jesus in His Revelation, which was received by Him from His Father after His ascension and then delivered to John, fills in a lot of the details of what both Daniel and Jesus are addressing here.

In *verses 16–20,* Jesus gives instructions for the escape from the city and, in fact, from all of Judea, to the mountains. Jesus tells them to pray that the flight be not in winter or on the Sabbath.

Then *in verses 21 and 22* Jesus tells why they must watch for the sign; flee when they see it, and pray for good conditions during their flight, *"For then there shall be Great Tribulation, such as has not been since the beginning of the world until this time, no, nor ever shall be and unless those days were shortened, no flesh would be saved; but for the elect's sake those days will be shortened."* These verses describe the days *after* the *desecration of the Temple in the middle of the End of Age Tribulation.* They describe a time that is far worse than the human race has ever experienced. These days are, indeed, The Great Tribulation, as these Scriptures declare them to be.

Verses 23–28 reveal that, these days will also be filled with lying wonders, deception and confusion, but also remember that *Verse 13* promises, *"But he who endures to the end will be saved."*

In *Verse 29* Jesus says, *"Immediately after The Tribulation of those days the sun will be darkened, and the moon will not give its light, the stars will fall from heaven, and the powers of the heavens will be shaken."* This shaking of the powers of heaven is *the sixth sign* of those signs that foretell the *beginning* and the *end* of The Tribulation. The first five signs, which are recorded in verse 7, are the beginning of sorrows as verse 8 says. *This sixth sign heralds its end.*

All that is recorded *between* the five beginning signs and this sixth sign, from *Verse 7* to *Verse 29* describe the events that occur *during* The Final Tribulation that really gets underway only after *the five beginning signs, the birth pains,* begin. Remember this when we read Luke's far different account.

Immediately after the sixth sign, the return of Jesus *brings The Tribulation to an end.* The culminating acts of the age are foretold in *verses 30 and 31,*

"Then the sign of the Son of Man will appear in heaven, and then all the tribes of the earth will mourn, and they will see the Son Of Man coming on the clouds of heaven with power and great glory and He will send His angels with a great sound of a trumpet, and they will gather together His elect from the four winds, from one end of heaven to the other."

These verses, 30 and 31, conclude the *very short history of the world* that the Holy Spirit has delivered to us through God's apostle and prophet, Matthew. *Matthew's history begins very late and is only about seven years long.*

It starts with the five signs that herald the beginning of The End of The Age Tribulation it ends *immediately* after this Tribulation has run its course with the coming of Jesus and the End of The Age.

Now let us examine *Luke's very different record*, the truth of which our ancient foe has tried so successfully to hide by twisting, braiding and blending it into Matthew's story to make the two stories appear as if they were one.

But know this *first* that no prophecy of Scripture is of any private interpretation. Just as *Matthew* wrote, *Luke* also wrote as he was moved by the Holy Spirit. We cannot discount *Luke's* record without great peril to our understanding of what *Jesus actually said* and to our own souls.

Luke wrote especially to the Gentile Christians of the first and the final generations, and of course, also to the believers of every age. He did not specifically write to the Jews, to those who, as Paul wrote in Romans 11, would be blinded in part until The Tribulation At The End Of This Age. That assignment was given to Matthew. Luke had a different job.

There are four different gospels for very good reasons!

However, church scholars, starting at least with Augustine in the fourth century, discounted Luke's record, counting it in error, whenever it appeared to them to be in conflict with Matthew. They also bent or discounted Matthew in favor of Luke when that seemed to work better. They had to do this to make the two records match each other since they contended that both records addressed the same events. Their contention was that the Great Tribulation centered on Jerusalem described in *Matthew 24:15–22* was the same event as the Destruction of Jerusalem described in *Luke 21:20–24*.

Achieving this particular equation of identity of events was the main means of taking the promises of God from the Jews and giving them to the Church. You see, if these two events are taken as a single event that can be proved to have occurred in 70 AD, then a host of related postulates can be sustained including:

- *That God finished His interference in the plans of men in history at that time* and it has been up to man and his church ever since to finish the work of God on earth. He is through and won't be back for a long, long time, if ever, for all practical purposes.
- *That we are now living in God's millenium and have been since A.D. 70, and that Satan is bound.*
- *That most of what Jesus said on the Mount of Olives was very symbolic and not useful history or trustworthy prophecy at all.*
- *That God was forever through with the Jews* and that which Paul wrote in chapters 9, 10, and 11 of the Letter to the Romans and many other Old and New Testament Scriptures relative to the place and role of Jerusalem and of the Jews at the end of the age is also only symbolic. And whatever promises and prerogatives Israel once had, now belong to the church.
- *That there remain no unfulfilled Prophecies* in the Bible except for His sudden and unexpected return as a thief in the night on judgment day.

It was apparently thought that by *silencing* God's word in Luke's Account, and twisting Matthew's it would be possible to obscure the facts that the records are quite different and that both recorders got it right. And that, in fact, Jesus had foretold two totally separate series of events spanning the entire history of the world from His day until the now approaching End Of The Age including two separate Desolations of Jerusalem, one done and one yet to come.

In addition to the grand larceny committed against the Jews, there have been other serious impacts of this disinformation down through the ages and especially even in our own generation. But these have already been noted and will be further amplified in *Part III, But Before All These Things.*

Now let us look at *Luke's 21st chapter record (The Very Different Story.)*

In verses *10 and 11* Luke also records the same five signs that herald the beginning of The Tribulation that Matthew does, but Luke, without a break or even a mention of the events of the *End Time Tribulation, immediately records the sixth sign*, which heralds the *end* of the *End Time Tribulation*. It is as if Luke's audience doesn't need to know the interior details of this Tribulation that Matthew so labored over (for 21 verses) for his audience! Why? *Because Luke's audience won't be here during the Tribulation*!

Then Luke, in *verse 12*, begins a list of all of the things that the disciples must experience *before* the *five signs* that signal the start of *The Final Tribulation* can begin. This list in Luke superficially resembles the events that Matthew says will occur *during The Final Tribulation*, but according to Jesus, all of the events of Luke's Record must occur *before The Signs of The Beginning of This Final Tribulation* can even begin!

This is evident from the text itself, which plainly says in *verse 12* (the Verse Satan has so effectively hidden) that these events in Luke's Account come *before* the signs of *The Final Tribulation* can even begin. It is also evident from the fact that most of These Prophecies of Jesus are also *recorded as fulfilled* in The New Testament in the very lifetime of the generation to which He was then speaking just as He also said they would be in *Matthew, chapter 23*. Whereas the Olivet Discourse Tribulation Events that are recorded in *Matthew chapter 24* plainly come after the first five signs that herald This Final Tribulation and are thus *End Of The Age Events, not first century events. And they haven't happened yet.*

The *fulfillment of the earliest of these prophecies* found in Luke's Record is recorded in the New Testament, itself, especially in the Book of Acts. The *fulfillment of the next earliest events* are recorded as being fulfilled in 70 AD in the writings of Josephus, specifically in his *Wars of the Jews*.

In *verses 12–19* Jesus tells them the things they will face in their own lifetime and how God will be with them. He prophesies their martyrdom and their deliverance, even as He later, in fact,

41

fulfilled these promises, for example, by delivering Stephen, receiving him into heaven even as he died, fulfilling His fantastic promise, *"They will put some of you to death...but not a hair of your head shall be lost."* Or as Paul vouchsafed for all of us who believe, *"Absent in the body, present with the Lord"*

> *Hallelujah saints! Amen!*

In verses 20 and 21 He says, *"But when you see Jerusalem surrounded by armies, then know that its desolation is near. Then let those who are in Judea flee to the mountains..."* This is not the same as the event prophesied in Matthew, verse 15, simply because this is not an end time event as the one in Matthew obviously is. It is a first generation event. We know this because it was fulfilled in 70 AD, within 38 years of the day in which Jesus spoke it. And we know this is not an end time event because this destruction of Jerusalem is in the list of the events that must come *before* the signs of the End Time Tribulation can *even begin*!

> The precise fulfillment of *Jesus' prophecies* in the first generation tells the final generation just how precisely they can expect *His prophecies* to be fulfilled for them in their very own lives!

The End Time Tribulation, itself will contain in its very center and heart the sign of The Abomination Of Desolation standing in the Holy Place, spoken of first by Daniel and now, by Jesus. This sign will herald the beginning of the worst of all Tribulations ever faced by mankind. It will be centered on Jerusalem in the second half of The Tribulation, but will be worldwide. *It is yet to come* and again the readers are urged *"to flee to the mountains of Judea."*

We also know that Luke speaks of the 70 AD destruction, not the one at the End of The Age as Matthew does because Jesus did not come in the clouds with power and great glory to end the limited tribulation of those days. The sixth sign did *not* appear and His sign did *not* appear in heaven and His angels did *not* gather the elect from the four winds, from one end of heaven to the other as *Matthew's Record* reports will all occur, in a time yet to come.

There are two destructions of Jerusalem prophesied on the Mount of Olives By Jesus:
- One in *His very own generation*, signaled by Encircling Armies, Scribed by Luke.
- One in the middle of the *still-in-our-future* End of The Age Tribulation signaled by a very different sign, *"The Abomination Of Desolation standing in the holy place,"* scribed by Matthew.

To make these two as if they were one, which is what the foe has attempted, and the church has believed, totally distorts the scriptures, prophecy, history, and the future. It makes total confusion out of what Jesus was trying to tell us and robs Him of the acclaim as the great I Am, the only one who can tell the end from the beginning. It also robs the Jews of the promises of God for their nation and has robbed many Christians of their promise of the kingdom of righteousness, peace and joy in the Holy Spirit. Did the harmonizers have all of these objectives in mind as they bent to do their work for the foe?

But to continue, *Luke* in *verse 22* gives the reason for this early destruction of Jerusalem, *"For these are the days of vengeance, that all things which are written may be fulfilled."* This is in agreement with Jesus' prophetic words as recorded in the condemnation of *Matthew 23:31–39*. In this condemnation He says, *"on you may come all the righteous blood shed on the earth. Assuredly, I say to you, all these things will come upon this generation."* And, of course, 38 years later they did, just as *it is written* that they would.

In Verse 23 Jesus again expresses great concern over the hardship of the escape. And He characterizes the conditions of the time as *"great distress in the land and wrath upon this people."*

And it hasn't happened yet! *But it will.* Jerusalem was destroyed and approximately 1,100,000 Jews died within its walls during the siege and another 97,000 or so were lead away captive to die in the arenas of Roman cities. This sounds bad enough, until it is compared to the holocaust of this past generation, when 6,000,000 Jews died. The holocaust sounds bad enough until it is compared to Matthew's account of *"the*

Great Tribulation such as has not been, since the beginning of the world until this time, nor ever shall be."

No, Luke's description of the destruction of 70 AD is of a limited area and a limited people. Matthew's is worldwide and the worst ever to happen.

The death and destruction Prophesied in Luke has already been exceeded.

The death and destruction prophesied in Matthew will not be exceeded ever.

In verse 24 Jesus declares the fate of Jerusalem in 70 AD and tells what will follow its destruction, and it is *not* the End of the Age and His immediate return as was the case in Mathew's telling. Instead, He says the fall of Jerusalem will be followed by events that have turned out to be *the very accurate history of the world from that day to this very generation!*

He said, *"And they shall fall by the edge of the sword and be led away captive into all nations. And Jerusalem will be trampled by Gentiles until the times of the Gentiles are fulfilled."* The *last half of this verse 24 prophecy* stretches out nearly two thousand years and reaches to this generation. The European Gentile nations, commencing their domination of the world under Alexander The Great, have reached their zenith in this our own generation (their times are fulfilled) and the prophesied parallel event in this half verse of the removal of the trampling boot occurred on June 7, 1967.

When you get to the last part of verse 24, *"and Jerusalem will be trampled by Gentiles until the times of the Gentiles are fulfilled."* Stop and think about it. It is astounding! It is as if the whole of the human race has conspired together for two thousand years to wipe the Jews off the face of the earth, even out of their hiding places in the most remote corners of the globe and then can neither foresee nor prevent their return and conquest of the very center of the earth and of its history, Jerusalem, *just as Jesus said they would!* The world could have known the outcome of all these campaigns, if they had just read the story that Jesus told, *just as He told it.*

It is also of *urgent* interest to this generation that all of the events that Luke's record declares must precede the beginning of the signs of the end have all now taken place, *the last of these events, the removal of the trampling Gentile boot from Jerusalem, in our lifetime!*

There is now nothing left on Jesus' prophetic timetable that has not been fulfilled that must be fulfilled before the signs of the end of the age begin. The signs of end can now begin at any time.

Or have they begun already? If they have already begun, faintly, as the first pains of labor, just as Jesus described them, we should be looking up for Jesus to fulfill His promise to take the believers up and out of here at any time now.

This is why He urges us to understand the season and to be ready. This is why He urges us to watch and pray.

Pay attention. I didn't make this up. It is in the *word*. It is written. This is no dream. This is no illusion and this is certainly no fabrication by anyone.

Now without any further mention of the five beginning signs of The Tribulation, nor any note of the terrible seven years that follow them; Luke in *verses 25 and 26* reintroduces the sixth sign, which signals the end of The Tribulation and Jesus' return. The sixth sign is mentioned again at this point in Luke for the dual purposes of signifying the end of the telling of all of the events that must all come before the signs of the end can commence and for setting the stage for The End of the Age *verse 27.*

It is of utmost significance that neither here nor in *verses 10 and 11* where all six signs are first given is there *any* word in Luke's account, whatsoever, of the horrible events of The Final Tribulation that lie between the first five signs and the sixth sign on which Matthew's account so intensely focuses. Even as Matthew does not say a word about *any* event (including the destruction of Jerusalem in 70 AD) that *precedes* the signs of the Beginning of The Tribulation, Luke gives us *no account, whatsoever, of what happens during* The final great End of the Age Tribulation. On one hand Matthew's audience isn't listening, on the other hand Luke's audience doesn't need instruction. They won't be here.

Verse 27, "Then they will see the Son of Man coming in a cloud with power and great glory." These are the same words as Matthew 30.

Both accounts now arrive at the same point in history. Luke by way of concentrating the weight of his record of Jesus' prophetic word on the trials, and victories of the first generation and Matthew by way of concentrating his record of Jesus' prophetic words on the End of Age Tribulation of the final generation. Both records are by the appointment of the Holy Spirit.

From this point on in the narrative the two records are synchronous, *but they still address two different audiences*, the Jews and other tardy believers in Matthew and the early believers in Luke.

To emphasize what we have learned to this point: These two *time lines* of Matthew and Luke are sequential and complementary as the Scriptures plainly set them out to be. They are not parallel nor are they the retelling of the same story. Taken together, sequential, as the Holy Scriptures present them; they cover the whole period of history from the day they were spoken until the end of this present age. These two accounts tie together chronologically at The Signs of The Beginning of The End of Days Tribulation, which are recorded in both accounts.

Beginning with verse 12, Luke tells of the events that *all must come before* the signs of the beginning of the end. *Beginning with verse 9, Matthew* tells of the events that *all will follow after* the signs of the beginning of the end.

Now, a careful reading of the few remaining verses of these two accounts will show that the early believers *will escape the final trials*, just as the believers who took God at his word as they found it in Luke's Record also escaped entrapment in Jerusalem in 70 AD. The late believers who are trapped here below in The Tribulation are encouraged in Matthew in the middle of The Tribulation to flee to the mountains and to endure to the end for their salvation. *Luke's early faithful are not told to run and hide or to endure the great affliction!*

No, they are told in verse 28 *"Now when these things (the first five signs) begin to happen, look up and lift up your heads, because your redemption draws near."* The faithful don't flee anywhere. He is coming for them to take them out. As soon as the five signs begin to appear His own are on notice that He is at the door to snatch them away before the coming Tribulation.

They are, however, instructed to *"Take heed to yourselves, lest your hearts be weighed down with carousing, drunkenness, and cares of this life, and that Day come on you unexpectedly. For it will come as a snare on all those who dwell on the face of the whole earth."* Jesus will catch up the believers before the trap is slammed shut and take them home to be with Him forever. In fact, the believers being caught up is the *slamming of the trap* for all of those left here below on the face of the earth just as the shutting of the door of Noah's Ark sealed the fate of the unbelievers of that generation.

> *Watch therefore and pray always that you may be counted worthy **to escape all these things that will come to pass, and to stand before the Son of Man.***

Then finally at the end of the story that Jesus told on The Mount Of Olives, *Jesus swears that the beginning of the Signs of the End, The Tribulation and His return will all occur within a single generation, just as He had also prophesied that the first destruction of Jerusalem would also occur within a single generation.*

Jesus then seals this final promise of the *brevity of the trial* of the final generation with an *awesome triune oath* in *Matthew 24:34–35, Mark 13:30–31* and *Luke 21:32–33.*

This oath-sealed promise of Jesus will be a sturdy support for the faith of all who must endure the time of Jacob's trouble to the end, here below, on the face of the earth.

This oath-promise encompasses a similar oath also sent from heaven concerning the duration of the Great Tribulation which is found in *Daniel 12:7.* Daniel's audience of Jews is the same as Matthew's. In Daniel they are only warned and promised about the duration of the second half of the final tribulation called by

Matthew, The Great Tribulation, because that is the last and greatest trial they must endure if they miss the rapture. That is the trial that comes after the Abomination of Desolation stands in the Holy Place, spoken of by Daniel and by Jesus. Jesus' Triune Oath expands the scope of the promise of limited duration of The Tribulation to a full generation to include the signs of the approach of The Tribulation. This is done for the hope and comfort of those who will escape before The Tribulation begins in earnest, but who must live to see the onset of the beginning of sorrows. We know they will see them because the beginning of these sorrows will be the very signal that their redemption is near.

Again because of the vital importance to the final generation of this promise by Jesus to shorten the Tribulation, we will study this promise and its unparalleled confirming oath in further detail in the section called *The Promise*.

Rapture Review

Before we leave the story that Jesus told on the mount let us look one more time to see if He left us any clues as to who will be taken up and away at His call and when, and who will be left behind to endure the Tribulation. Let's review what we have just read from the perspective of just these two questions.

In both Mathew and Luke, Jesus sets out the *six signs* that will mark out the beginning and the end the terrible time of the end. The first five signs herald the *beginning* of this great time of testing. The *sixth and final sign* heralds the *end* of the ordeal.

Luke describes to the early believers all of the events that come before the first five signs of the end; Matthew describes to the late believers all of the events that come after the first five signs of the end. In *Matthew's account*: the *first five of these signs* are called, *"the beginning of sorrows"*, as verse 8 says. *These first five signs* are: *"nation will arise against nation, kingdom against kingdom, famines and pestilences and earthquakes in various places"*. Matthew doesn't introduce the *sixth sign* until verse 29. *This sixth sign* is the signal of the end of the great tribulation. It is summed up as, *"and the powers of the heavens will be shaken"*. In Matthew's account, all of the verses between, Verses 9–28, are devoted to describing the terrible things that are going to take place *during* The Tribulation. The purpose of the foretelling of these events is obviously to help those who live on earth during these times to survive them, if at all possible and to persevere until the end for their salvation. But a great secondary purpose is to *warn and motivate* those who read *(and believe)* this account *early enough* to escape these times altogether.

Luke's account, unlike Matthew's, does not break the end time signs into two parts. He describes the five signs *heralding the beginning of the end days tribulation*, similar to the way Matthew does, but then without a break, he immediately describes *the sixth sign, "fearful sights and great signs from heaven,"* which heralds *the end* of the final days of the age. Amazingly, Luke gives *no* account of the horrendous events that lie *between* the first five signs of *the beginning*, and the sixth sign of *the end* of these days of unsurpassed tribulation. He simply runs all six signs together, *as if nothing happens between the fifth and sixth sign.* He skips seven years of history. The terrible events which, in fact, take place between the *fifth and six sign, are recorded in full detail in Matthew24: 9–28 and in many other places in the Scriptures,* both the Old and New Testaments. *But they are not found in Luke 21. Not one word in Luke's record describes a single event, which occurs during The Tribulation! Why?*

Matthew was written primarily for the Jews and this primary audience hasn't even read it yet, even at this late date! They will read it with great fervor *during* The Tribulation and will need all the succor, hope and guidance it offers for these terrible times. Luke, on the other hand, was written primarily for the Gentiles and these early believers will escape these final days *entirely*, by simply reading, *believing and heeding* His early warnings. They won't be pouring over these details in Matthew. They will be gone. Jesus will have taken them home. *The beginning of the birth pains of The Tribulation is the sign that He gives them notifying them of their soon departure.*

In *Luke 21:28* Jesus comforts the faithful and encourages them to trust Him and to stand steady, for the rapture is at hand. He says, *"when these things begin to come to pass then look up, and lift up your heads for your redemption draweth nigh."*

The Specific Events Compared

Jesus described two separate sets of events on the Mount of Olives that would occur nearly two thousand years apart. One set is clearly recorded by Luke as happening before the signs of the approach of the end of the age. And the other set is clearly recorded by Matthew as happening after the signs of the approach of the end of the age. But, even if the radical oversight is made of missing the two sequence-ordering verses of 9 and 12, a careful study of the event-descriptive verse Scriptures, 9–29 and 12–24, paired in these two chapters and taught by some to be describing the same events, will show that they do not describe the same events at all.

To appreciate the sometimes subtle and some times bold, differences in the descriptions of these two separate series of events, let us address these verses in some detail: First, the events that precede the desolations of Jerusalem; second, the desolations of Jerusalem; third, the events that follow after the desolations of Jerusalem, and fourth; the timing of the end. Let's get our *Bibles* out.

Events leading up to the desolations of Jerusalem

This section compares the events leading up to the destruction that took place in 70 AD which are foretold by Jesus in *Luke 21:12–19* and the events leading up to the desolation that will take place during The Tribulation of the last days which are prophesied by Jesus in *Matthew 24:9–14*.

The events foretold in Luke's account in these verses are exactly what Jesus foretold in many other places would be the experience of the early church. Study *John 14:25–26; 15:18–19, 26–27; 16:1–2 & 13* and *Acts 1:8* among many other Scriptures.

The Book of Acts then records that just such events did, in fact, happen to the early church, just as Jesus prophesied. For examples of this, look at *Acts 4; 5:17–42; 6:8–15, & 7* and many other places. Read these Scriptures for a perfect example of prophecy spoken - prophecy fulfilled.

Specifically, as Jesus foretold, the Christians were brought before synagogues and rulers to bear witness to the resurrection and the gospel. They would not have to prepare what they were to say. God would give them a mouth that could not be overcome. He said they should not worry about what to say, that the Holy Spirit would put the words in their mouth. and He did.

They would be hated for His name's sake. And although some would be killed, *"not a hair of their head would perish!"* This astonishing prophecy, found in verse 18, is a bulwark of the faith of the saints of all ages. It is not so difficult to understand, *and believe*, because from the very beginning God illustrated it for us. It was so wonderfully shown to us in its first fulfillment in the life, death and life of Stephen, the very first to receive this promise. Just before his death he was given a view into the presence of God *and* he reported it. Luke records it in *Acts 7:55–56*, "But being filled with the Holy Spirit he gazed intently into heaven and saw the glory of God, and Jesus standing at the right hand of God; and he said, *'Behold, I see the heavens opened up and the Son of Man standing at the right hand of God,'* or as Paul would vouchsafe for himself and for the rest of us "Absent in the body, Present with the Lord." Although Stephen was killed, not a hair of his head perished. He passed from death to life, even as all Christians do when they fall asleep in Jesus. Believe, Christian. This is the Gospel. This is our greatest hope and our joy. Study *I Corinthians 15 and I Thessalonians 4* to refresh your souls.

Although these were severe times of great testing, they were also times of great purpose, great victories and great joy. Yes, Luke describes the first glorious days of faith and the great outpouring of the Spirit and the bold joy of the early disciples as they fearlessly followed their Lord in the very paths that He had prophesied they would walk in. These were not tribulation times, but the glorious and joyous and victorious times of the first declaration of the gospel of Jesus Christ by men.

In contrast, Matthew's account in verses 7–14 foretells the first half of the last terrible days of the Jews (and the world). The Jews as a people will be hated by all nations for His name's sake. (As surely as the nations have hated the Jews because of Jesus during all these intervening years, that hatred will abound in the final days of The Tribulation.) In addition, the Jews who become Christians will receive a double measure of the hatred of the unbelievers, Jews and Gentiles alike. Mutual betrayal and hatred, iniquity abounding and love waxed cold, false prophets and deceptions will abound in the society of the last days as Matthew says, and Paul confirms in his prophecy of the last days in *II Timothy Chapter 3*.

However, there will be those, the elect, the remnant, Jews and Gentiles, alike, who will come to the Lord in The Tribulation. The recovery of the *Jewish Remnant* by means of the fiery trial of the final tribulation is a theme of both the New and the Old Testament and is especially foretold in *Daniel 12, Romans 11, Matthew 24:22, Revelation 6:9–11* and *Revelation chapters 7 & 14.*

God chose The Tribulation as the closing epoch of this age for the very purpose of purifying, making white and refining His people, the Jew first and also the Gentile. He chastises the sons whom He loves. He desires that no man be lost. In the midst of the firestorm He sends His prophets and His evangelists once again, for one last time to Proclaim salvation. By God's own definition this is an end time proclamation, not the story of 70 AD.

Luke, in these verses, is clearly telling the story of the first adventures of the first Christians of the first generation.

Matthew, in these verses, is clearly telling the story of the first half of the end of the days tribulation of the Jews and of the whole world. His is the story of the beginning of the end for the final generation.

> "This **Gospel of the Kingdom** will be preached in all the world as a witness to all nations, **and then the end will come.**" Matt. 24:14

The Desolations of Jerusalem

This section compares the destruction of Jerusalem by Titus in 70 AD as foretold by Jesus in *Luke 21:20–24a* and the coming desolation of Jerusalem by the antichrist at the mid point of the final tribulation as foretold by Jesus in *Matthew 24:15–28*.

All Bible students agree that Luke tells the story of the destruction of Jerusalem by Titus and his Roman legions in 70 AD. Sadly, most churches that derive their traditions and doctrines from the state churches of Rome and Constantinople wrongly teach that Matthew's account in chapter 24 is of this same destruction. The old state churches had a vital vested interest in teaching this error, which we will explore later.

Most American churches today, got what they teach about history and the end times, not from the Scriptures, but from these old state church traditions. Some of these churches today are *Roman Catholic, Eastern Orthodox, Episcopalian, Methodists, Presbyterian, Lutheran*, the *Restoration Movement churches* and many of the derivatives of all of these groups. Doctrinal cross breeding has even affected groups, which are not so tightly tied to these traditions on most other issues.

God's Different Purposes in the Two Desolations

In 70 AD.

In *Matthew 23* in His public proclamation, (not in His private discourse with His disciples on the Mount Of Olives recorded in Matthew 24) Jesus does tell the nature, the time and the purpose of the destruction of Jerusalem in 70 AD. He says she will be left desolate, that this desolation will occur in *that generation*, and that it will be in retribution for all of the innocent blood spilled in her, or as Jesus says in Luke's record, "For these are the days of vengeance, that all things which are written may be fulfilled." or to paraphrase Josephus, "that the evil had become so great in the city that if

Again, we have *prophecy spoken - prophecy fulfilled. Praise* and *thanks be to God* for Josephus for the record of the fulfillment.

the Romans had not destroyed it, God would have had to find some other way to do the job". The destruction of the city in 70 AD had no redeeming value other than that which was accomplished in the destruction of Sodom and Gomorrah, that is, to do justice for crimes committed and to rid a very special part of the world of sin, at least temporarily.

In The Final Days.

The purpose of the coming desolation of Jerusalem in the final tribulation is quite different. In *Daniel 12*, the purpose of the final trouble is declared to be the refining, purifying and redeeming of the Remnant. His elect will be delivered, but it will be from a nation that is totally shattered.

Different Signs

In *Luke 21:20*, the sign given for the coming destruction of Jerusalem was "Jerusalem compassed by armies". Although the timing and the circumstances of the damnation of Jerusalem in 70 AD are assuredly foretold by Jesus' in *Luke 19:41–44* and *Mathew 23:31–39*, this is the *only* sign given by Jesus of that impending doom for the purpose of facilitating the escape of the Saints.

In 70 AD the Romans completed the encirclement of Jerusalem, hemming in all of the citizens of Israel who had fled to the city as the refuge of last resort. Fearful and impatient Christians must have wondered what kind of sign Jesus had given them, because they couldn't very well flee with the city surrounded. When the Romans lifted the siege for a brief time, for reasons those in the city didn't understand, the relieved Christians took the sign as from God, which it was, and fled to the hills as instructed and escaped. The non-believing Jews celebrated the unexpected victory that they believed they had achieved. Then the circle closed again and there was no escape for them. All of those who didn't *know, believe and act* on the words of Jesus recorded in *Luke 21:20* either perished in the city or later in the arenas of cities all across the Roman Empire.

In 70 AD the Temple was not desecrated by a blasphemous idol being placed in the Holy Place. The Romans were very superstitious. They feared the God of the Jews. They would not have dared to do such a thing. Instead, the Temple was accidentally burned down either by the Jews or Romans. No one knows today who started the fire or for what purpose. What is clear, however, is that the Temple fire began long after the siege circle was completed, the city walls breached and the slaughter begun.

In trying to equate Matthew's destruction to Luke's, some say that the fire or even the assembly of the Roman Legions' standards on the Temple Mount after the battle were what Daniel and Jesus referred to as the "abomination of desolation". The major problem with this obviously contrived construction is that these "signs" occurred much too late in the siege to be a useful sign to flee to the mountains.

In *Matthew 24:15–16*, the sign given was, *"When ye therefore shall see the abomination of desolation, spoken of by Daniel the prophet, stand in the Holy Place, (whoever reads, let him understand) then let those who are in Judea flee to the mountains."*

In Jesus' days in the flesh the Jews had long believed that the Syrian Antiochus IV had already fulfilled *Daniel's prophecies* about "the abomination of desolation and the stopping of the daily sacrifices." *And he had!*

It is fascinating that Matthew (and Mark) instructed by the Holy Spirit, inserted words in Jesus' discourse at this point to emphasis to the reader the importance of Jesus' reference to the prophet Daniel. This is the only God-authorized comment on Jesus' words in all of the records of the Olivet Discourse.

It must be a very important comment!

What is it that the reader is to understand about Daniel's prophecy?

Actually Daniel mentions the "abomination of desolation standing in the Holy Place" not once, but four times: in *Daniel*

8:13, 9:27, 11:31 & 12:11. In all four passages "the taking away of the daily sacrifices" is also mentioned along with the setting up of the "abomination of desolation in the Holy Place". This suggests not just a temporary, one time, desecration of the temple, but an intention to permanently and fundamentally change the religion of the people.

Antiochus IV Epiphanies did this very thing in 168 BC, killing the priests, sacrificing a pig on the altar, and setting up a statue of the Greek god Zeus in the Holy Place, totally outlawing Judaism and replacing it with Greek pantheism and philosophy. His purpose was to rid the world of Jewish superstitions and force the Jews, and all others, to accept the enlightened, tolerant (except for the worship of Jehovah), modern, and reasonable culture of the Greeks. This Greek culture had already shown its superiority over all other cultures, had it not? Does this sound familiar? Can you see a replay of this coming?

The only problem was that the obstinate Jews resisted what was good for them. They revolted against the Greek Seleucid rulers of Syria, one of the super powers of the time. This revolt led by the Maccabees ended with the defeat of the vastly superior army of the Greeks and the cleansing and rededication of the Temple by the Jews exactly three years later.

To honor this event the Jews celebrate the Feast of Dedication to this very day as the Festival of Lights at Christmas time. It is recorded in *John 10:22* that Jesus was in Jerusalem on the Feast of Dedication and on that very special day, 25 Chesliv (about December 25!) in the Temple, He first declared that He was the Christ.

Now Jesus is telling them that the fulfillment is yet to be! No wonder Matthew is telling them (and us) to understand. In light of this urging let us pay closer attention.

Let the reader understand!

The four references in Daniel to the "abomination of desolation" share a curious similarity: In each case, the "abomination of desolation" is set in an historical sequence, prophetically foretold.

57

Even more striking is that the second and fourth references, *Daniel 9:27 & 12:11,* are given as time markers of the coming of the end of the age, in just the same way that Jesus used it. However, in contrast to Jesus' teachings in Matthew and Mark where he doesn't identify the length of time between the sign and the culmination of the age, both of these two references in Daniel set out the exact time that will elapse between the sign and certain final events of the end of the age. Several end events are indicated in Daniel that we do not yet understand, but what we do understand is that they will come to pass in a little over three and a half years after the blasphemy takes place. Jesus did not repeat this vital information concerning the duration of the horrible end time events, which information had already been delivered by a prophet of God. He simply referenced it! Matthew and Mark wrote, *"Let the reader understand."*

Obviously since the end did not occur in about $3\,{}^1/_2$ years after 70 AD Jesus is not referring in Matthew to the destruction of Jerusalem in 70 AD by Titus. But to a destruction that is yet to be. It will occur approximately three and a half years before the end of the age, if we understand Daniel. In the final days, the mystery of the exact time, exact to the very day, will be understood. *Daniel 12:10* says, *"The wise will understand."* Matthew and Mark say, *"Let the reader understand."*

The first and third references, *Daniel 8:13 & 11:31,* are set in a series of prophesied events that turned out to be such an accurate account of the life and deeds of Antiochus IV that doubters of a later age discounted the Book of Daniel as fraudulent, written after the fact, simply recording history that had already taken place. However, whether doubters or believers, all testify that this writing concerns Antiochus IV. So, even the doubters and scoffers agree with the believers on this point. What a wonder! And what does it mean? The impact of this universally accepted fact is that in Antiochus IV we have a perfect model of the antichrist and his actions. Let the reader understand what Antiochus IV did will be done again and recognizably in the same way. There will be a temple that will be desecrated by the abomination of desolation that will stand in the Holy Place. The daily sacrifices will be taken away. In 539 BC Daniel said it would be done. In 168 BC Antiochus IV did it. In 32 AD Jesus said, it will be done. In 70 AD Titus did not do it. According to Daniel 3 $^1/_2$ years before the end, it will be done. *Let the reader understand.*

In Summary, we understand from Daniel that the blasphemy will take place, about three and a half years before Jesus returns at the end of the age. We also understand that its form will not be an encircling army but a Zeus type statue standing in the Holy Place. Jesus said it would be as Daniel spoke of it. Matthew and Mark said, "Let the reader understand."

The events following the desolations of Jerusalem

In *Luke 21:24* we read *"And they shall fall by the edge of the sword. And shall be lead away captive into all nations: and Jerusalem shall be trodden down of the Gentiles until the times of the Gentiles be fulfilled."* This is the sum total of Luke's account of all of the events that would follow the first destruction of Jerusalem in 70 AD, from its destruction up until the signs that herald the approach of the final days. What does it say? It says that for some indefinite period of time after the fall of Jerusalem, Gentiles will dominate Jerusalem. Then the Gentiles will not dominate Jerusalem, meaning, of course, the return of the Jews to Jerusalem. Then all six signs will occur and the Lord will return. That is it. There are no details. But, what is revealed does take us up to the present day.

In contrast in *Matthew 24:21 & 22* we read that after the desecration of the temple that the greatest tribulation of all times, past and future, will occur. The Great Tribulation will certainly be fiercer, more intense and widespread than the death of the eleven hundred thousand Jews who perished in 70 AD. It will be harsher and greater even than the death of the six million Jews who perished in the holocaust during the thirties and forties of the twentieth century. It will be greater than The Tribulation that precedes the desecration of the Temple, which is detailed by Matthew in verses 9–14.

Although this terror is focused on Jerusalem, it will be worldwide. It will vastly exceed in devastation even the 40 to 60 million of all nations who died in WW II. It will occur in a short period of time. These are the words in *Matthew 24:21–22,*

"For then shall be great tribulation, such as was not since the beginning of the world to this time, no nor ever shall be. And except those days should be shortened, there should no flesh be saved: but for the elects sake those days shall be shortened." Matt. 24: 21, 22

This end time prophecy of unequaled General Destruction is in great contrast to the limited destruction that is identified in Luke's record and fulfilled in the events of 70 AD as declared in *Luke 21: 23*, "*—for there shall be great distress in the land and wrath upon this people.*" Not worldwide, just the land, this people; not greatest ever tribulation, just great distress.

Matthew's account of greatest ever-worldwide destruction, limited only by time, contrasts greatly with Luke's very limited "great distress." "the land" and "this people." In Luke's Account of 70 AD the devastation is essentially finished when Jerusalem falls. In Matthew, the real horror of the end of the age, The Great Tribulation, really begins after the Temple is desecrated.

Josephus gives us the gruesome details of the limited horror of 70 AD, a horror that has since been exceeded by the holocausts and wars of our own age. Jesus' revelation given to John fills in a lot of the details of this yet coming worst of all times and shows its worldwide impact. 70 AD is certainly not what Matthew is writing about.

Let the reader understand.

The timing of the end

Finally, let it be noted with great wonder that the timing of the very end events are described very differently in *Luke 21:24–27* and in *Matthew 24:21–31*.

In Matthew, the end comes immediately after the Great Tribulation with the return of Jesus. And it will.

In Luke, the end comes some time after the times of the Gentiles are fulfilled and the trampling boot is removed, many years after the first destruction of Jerusalem. And it will.

And again, Luke doesn't even mention the Great Tribulation, just the signs that announce its beginning and marks its end.

This is the end of the detailed comparison of the specific events associated with the signs of the end and how they differ as described in *Matthew 24: 9–28* and *Luke 21:12–24*.

And my, how they differ!

The Scriptures

Matthew 24 and Luke 21, side-by-side, high lighted texts

All that has been written before is simply an introduction to the following presentation of Matthew 24 and Luke 21, side by side, King James version, with high lighted texts. The purpose of this presentation is to make clear the relationship between the true end times signs, which are common to both accounts, and the distinctly separate series of events, which are then recorded in each account. Simultaneously trace these two accounts with your own fingers and your own eyes and ponder them in your heart.

The texts in this side-by-side presentation are printed in the following distinctive styles to aid in more easily discerning what Jesus was saying in these two accounts.

The true Signs which will foreshadow the beginning and herald the end of The Final Tribulation, in the middle of which the desolation of the Temple occurs and which is ended by His return and the end of the age (*Matthew 7,8 & 29* and *Luke 10,11, 25 & 26*) are all printed in *italic letters*. Note carefully all of these sign verses and where they occur in the texts. This is very important.

This is where my heart stumbled, but: This is *no misprint!* This is *no mistake by God!* This is *no illusion*! And this is *no dream.*

The greatly contrasting words and phrases which set forth the two opposite orders of sequence of the signs and events of *Matthew 24: 9*, "**<u>THEN,</u>**" & *Luke 21: 12*, "**<u>BUT BEFORE ALL THESE THINGS,</u>**" are printed in bold underlined capital letters. These are the key words for understanding the sequences of the events of these two chapters as they were prophesied and as they have taken place in history up to the present day and as they will take place to the end.

The sequence of events that in Matthew follow the signs (vs. 9–28) and in Luke come before the Signs (vs. 12–24) are printed in **bold** letters.

These two separate series of happenings, recorded in Matthew and Luke, when taken together in the order given by Jesus, reveal that there are two desolations of the Temple in Jerusalem. One has happened. One has not. There are two sets of trying events. One has been completed and is well documented in the Book of the Acts of the Apostles, the accounts of Josephus, early Christian writers and the archives of this generation's own wire services. The other *may* or *may not* have begun quite yet, but in all likelihood awaits this present generation.

Luke's series of events, which are all past history from the perspective of the time in which we now live, are also a kind of sign, themselves, that foreshadow the coming of the signs that foretell the final days. This is because the signs of the end, which precede the events of the final days, cannot even begin until Luke's preceding series of events is completed. And now it has been.

Luke's series of events ends with the last half of verse 24, *"Jerusalem will be trodden down of the Gentiles until the times of the Gentiles has been fulfilled."* This final event of the series, which is the necessary precursor to the beginning of the signs that precede the end, did not come to pass until this very generation in which we now live.

World history again testifies to the faithfulness of God. As He ordained, the Jews never disappeared in spite of Satan's world's persistent effort for nearly two thousand years to wipe them off the face of the earth. They, in fact, retook Jerusalem in June 1967 and removed the last of the Gentiles trampling boot,

Luke's preconditions have now been completed. The signs of the beginning of the final days of distress can now begin at any time. Or have they begun already as the first faint pains of labor? Watch and pray.

Just as *Jesus prophesied* in *Luke 21: 24* on the Mount of Olives in 32 AD.

There have always been nation against nation, kingdom against kingdom, famines, pestilences and earthquakes. However, even if the true signs of this age's closing events are distinctive, by an order of magnitude, from all that has gone before, it will still take careful watching and praying to discern the faint beginnings of the birthing pains of this sea change of world history in order to know that the time is near, at the very door.

As Luke admonishes in verses 28 and 34,

"And when these things begin to come to pass, then look up, and lift up your heads, for your redemption draweth nigh. Be on your guard, that your hearts may not be weighed down with dissipation and drunkenness and the worries of life, and that day come on you suddenly like a trap."

Finally, the Scriptures setting forth God's ultimate confirming and sealing *oath* about the timing of these climactic events are printed in **bold italic** letters. These unique and vital verses are addressed in both *The Analysis* and, especially in *The Promise*. Please invest some heavy-duty heart and mind time there.

Now let us go to: *The Word of God!*

Matthew 24 and Luke 21 Side By Side
King James Version with high lighted texts

Matthew

Chapter 24

1 Then Jesus went out, and departed from the temple: and His disciples came to Him for to shew Him the buildings of the temple.

2 And Jesus said unto them, See ye not all these things? verily I say unto you there shall not be left here one stone upon another, that shall not be thrown down.

3 And as He sat upon the mount of Olives, the disciples came unto Him privately, saying, Tell us, when shall these things be? and what shall be the sign of Thy coming, and of the end of the world?

4 And Jesus answered and said unto them, Take heed that no man deceive you.

5 For many shall come in my name, saying, I am Christ; and shall deceive many.

6 And ye shall hear of wars and rumors of wars: see that ye be

Luke

Chapter 21

1 And He looked up, and saw the rich men casting their gifts into the treasury.

2 And He saw also a certain poor widow casting in thither two mites.

3 And He said, Of a truth I say unto you, that this poor widow hath cast in more than they all:

4 For all these have of their abundance cast in unto the offerings of God: but she of her penury hath cast in all the living that she had.

5 And as some spoke of the Temple, how it was adorned with goodly stones and gifts, He said,

6 As for these things which ye behold, the days will come, in the which there shall not be left one stone upon another, that shall not be thrown down.

7 And they asked Him, saying, Master, but when shall these things be? and what sign will

Matthew

Chapter 24

not troubled: for all these things must come to pass, but the end is not yet.

7 *For nation shall rise against nation, and kingdom against kingdom: and there shall be famines, and pestilences, and earthquakes, in diverse places.*

8 *All these are the beginning of sorrows.*

9 **<u>THEN</u> shall they deliver you up to be afflicted, and shall kill you: and ye shall be hated of all nations for my name's sake.**

10 **And then shall many be offended, and shall betray one another, and shall hate one another.**

11 **And many false prophets shall rise, and shall deceive many.**

12 **And because iniquity shall abound, the love of many shall wax cold.**

13 **But he that shall endure unto the end, the same shall be saved.**

14 **And this gospel of the kingdom shall be preached in**

Luke

Chapter 21

there be when these things shall come to pass?

8 And He said, Take heed that ye be not deceived: for many shall come in My name saying, I am Christ; and the time draweth near: go ye not therefore after them.

9 But when ye shall hear of wars and commotions, be not terrified: for these things must first come to pass; but the end is not by and by.

10 *Then said He unto them, Nation shall rise against nation, and kingdom against kingdom:*

11 *And great earthquakes shall be in divers places, and famines, and pestilences; and fearful sights and great signs shall there be from heaven.*

12 **<u>BUT BEFORE ALL THESE</u>, they shall lay their hands on you, and persecute you, delivering you up to the synagogues, and into prisons, being brought before kings and rulers for My Name's sake.**

Matthew

Chapter 24

all the world for a witness unto all nations; and then shall the end come.

15 When ye therefore shall see the abomination of desolation, spoken of by Daniel the prophet, stand in the holy place, (whoso readeth, let him understand)

16 Then let them which be in Judea flee into the mountains:

17 Let him which is on the housetop not come down to take any thing out of his house:

18 Neither let him which is in the field return back to take his clothes.

19 And woe unto them that are with child, and to them that give suck in those days!

20 But pray ye that your flight be not in the winter, neither on the sabbath day:

21 For then shall be great tribulation, such as was not since the beginning of the world to this time, no, nor ever shall be.

Luke

Chapter 21

13 And it shall turn to you for a testimony.

14 Settle it therefore in your hearts, not to meditate before what ye shall answer:

15 For I will give you a mouth and wisdom, which all your adversaries shall not be able to gainsay nor resist.

16 And ye shall be betrayed both by parents, and brethren, and kinsfolk, and friends; and some of you shall they cause to be put to death.

17 And ye shall be hated of all men for my name's sake.

18 But there shall not an hair of your head perish.

19 In your patience possess ye your souls.

20 And when ye shall see Jerusalem compassed with armies, then know that the desolation thereof is nigh.

21 Then let them which are in Judaea flee to the mountains; and let them which are in the midst of it depart out; and let not them that are in the countries enter thereinto.

Matthew

Chapter 24

22 And except those days should be shortened, there should no flesh be saved: but for the elect's sake those days shall be shortened.

23 Then if any man shall say unto you, Lo, here is Christ, or there; believe it not.

24 For there shall arise false Christs, and false prophets, and shall shew great signs and wonders; insomuch that, if it were possible, they shall deceive the very elect.

25 Behold, I have told you before.

26 Wherefore if they shall say unto you, Behold, He is in the desert; go not forth: behold, He is in the secret chambers; believe it not.

27 For as the lightning cometh out of the east, and shineth even unto the west; so shall also the coming of the Son of Man be.

28 For wheresoever the carcass is, there will the eagles be gathered together.

Luke

Chapter 21

22 For these be the days of vengeance, that all things which are written may be fulfilled.

23 But woe unto them that are with child, and to them that give suck, in those days! for there shall be great distress in the land, and wrath upon this people.

24 And they shall fall by the edge of the sword, and shall be led away captive into all nations: and Jerusalem shall be trodden down of the Gentiles, until the times of the Gentiles be fulfilled.

25 *And there shall be signs in the sun, and in the moon, and in the stars; and upon the earth distress of nations, with perplexity; the sea and the waves roaring:*

26 *Men's hearts failing them for fear, and for looking after those things which are coming on the earth: for the powers of heaven shall be shaken.*

Matthew

Chapter 24

29 *Immediately after The Tribulation of those days shall the sun be darkened, and the moon shall not give her light, and the stars shall fall from heaven, and the powers of the heavens shall be shaken:*

30 And then shall appear the sign of the Son of Man in heaven: and then shall all the tribes of the earth mourn, and they shall see the Son of Man coming in the clouds of heaven with power and great glory.

31 And He shall send His angels with a great sound of a trumpet, and they shall gather together His elect from the four winds, from one end of heaven to the other.

32 Now learn a parable of the fig tree; When his branch is yet tender, and putteth forth leaves, ye know that summer is nigh:

33 So likewise ye, when ye shall see all these things, know that it is near, even at the doors.

34 *Verily I say unto you, This generation shall not pass, till all these things be fulfilled.*

Luke

Chapter 21

27 And then shall they see the Son of Man coming in a cloud with power and great glory.

28 And when these things begin to come to pass, then look up, and lift up your heads; for your redemption draweth nigh.

29 And He spoke to them a parable; Behold the fig tree, and all the trees;

30 When they now shoot forth, ye see and know of your own selves that summer is now nigh at hand.

31 So likewise ye, when ye see these things come to pass, know ye that the kingdom of God is nigh at hand.

32 *Verily I say unto you, This generation shall not pass away, till all be fulfilled.*

33 *Heaven and earth shall pass away: but My words shall not pass away.*

34 And take heed to yourselves, lest at any time your hearts be overcharged with surfeiting, and drunkenness, and cares of this life, and so that day come upon you unawares.

Matthew

Chapter 24

35 *Heaven and earth shall pass away, but My words shall not pass away.*

36 But of that day and hour knoweth no man, no, not the angels of heaven, but My Father only.

37 But as the days of Noah were, so shall also the coming of the Son of Man be.

38 For as in the days that were before the flood they were eating and drinking, marrying and giving in marriage, until the day that Noah into the ark,

39 And knew not until the flood came, and took them all away; so shall also the coming of the Son of Man be.

40 Then shall two be in the field; the one shall be taken, and the other left.

41 Two women shall be grinding at the mill; the one shall be taken, and the other left.

42 Watch therefore: for ye know not what hour your Lord doth come.

43 But know this, that if the goodman of the house had known in what watch the thief

Luke

Chapter 21

35 For as a snare shall it come on all them that dwell on the face of the whole earth.

36 Watch ye therefore, and pray always, that ye may be accounted worthy to escape all these things that shall come to pass, and to stand before the Son of Man.

37 And in the day time He was teaching in the temple; and at night He went out, and abode in the mount that is called the mount of Olives.

38 And all the people came early in the morning to Him in the temple, for to hear Him.

Matthew

Chapter 24

would come, he would have watched, and would not have suffered his house to be broken up.

44 Therefore be ye also ready: for in such an hour as ye think not the Son of Man cometh.

45 Who then is a faithful and wise servant, whom his Lord hath made ruler over His household, to give them meat in due season?

46 Blessed is that servant, whom his Lord when He cometh shall find so doing.

47 Verily I say unto you, That He shall make him ruler over all His goods.

48 But and if that evil servant shall say in his heart, my Lord delayeth His coming;

49 And shall begin to smite His fellow servants, and to eat and drink with the drunken;

50 The Lord of that servant shall come in a day when he looketh not for Him, and in an hour that he is not aware of,

51 And shall cut him asunder, and appoint him his portion with the hypocrites: there shall be weeping and gnashing of teeth.

The Analysis

The times and the signs of the desolations of the Jewish Temples in Jerusalem and God's special provisions for His people in these dreadful times

The Analysis is a detailed, in depth; verse-by-verse, side-by-side study of these two chapters of Matthew 24 and Luke 21 in table form. A prayerful study of *The Analysis* will make clear what God, from the beginning, has intended for us to know by this time (at the very latest). Many of today's most debated issues will have an uncommon light shed upon them by this study, including:

- The certainty of the identity of Jesus as Jehovah God
- The certainty of His direction of human history, from beginning to end, including, especially, the events of today
- The signs and events of the rapidly approaching final days
- Our responsibility to watch for, and discern these signs and events and to take the action that He prescribes for our salvation.
- The certainty of His early rescue of the faithful from the terrible things that will befall all those who dwell on the face of the earth by snatching them up suddenly and keeping them safe with Him during this dreadful time that will surpass all other times of human history in dread and horror
- His end-of-era dealing with the Jews, breaking them down physically to redeem them spiritually as promised in *Daniel 12*, but ending the horror just in time to save the precious remnant, from out of the midst of the refining fire

It is often noted that each of the Gospels appears to be addressed primarily to different audiences: Matthew to the Jew; Mark to the Roman; Luke to the Greek, and John, a second touch of grace to everyman.

The different requirements of these distinctive audiences are sometimes set forth as the very reason that *God* provided *four gospels* in the first place.

By careful study of the whole of the Olivet Discourse it will become a certainty to the reader that the accounts of Matthew and Luke are addressed to two different primary audiences. Luke is addressed primarily to the early believers and Matthew primarily to the late believers, mainly the Jews of the final days. This division of labor is evident throughout.

For example, Matthew 24 does not address any aspect of the tragedy of 70 AD because Matthew's predominately Jewish audience wasn't listening, as the subsequent history so sadly proved. God didn't waste valuable time and effort on those who would not hear.

In fact, practically no word of Matthew 24 is addressed to the Jew about the history of the world until the very end game of the age, which is now about to be played out and no offer is made even then of an early escape to his audience from these terrible latter times. Again they are not listening. However, then, in the midst of this, their ultimate travail, He gives them a sign, an instruction and a refuge and the encouragement to hang on, faithful to the end. According to Daniel, by this time the Jews are beginning to understand and to seek their God and their ever faithful God is there for them when they call on Him, or, as Jesus said, *"when they say, blessed is he who comes in the name of the Lord."* Then, of course, Matthew's account becomes very detailed and intense, echoing and reinforcing Daniel's prophecies of these very same times to this very same audience.

In contrast, Luke describes the early testimonies, persecutions and salvation of the Christians and the signs and instructions for their escape from the destruction of Jerusalem in the first century. History tells us that they heeded Luke's record and escaped.

Luke also gives the end-of-the-age Christians the signs of the end, as does Matthew, but, he gives no interior detail of the dreadful events of this final period, nor instructions to hang on nor to flee. It seems that it is sufficient for the salvation of Luke's audience to simply set out the signs that herald the beginning of this period!

This is because Jesus' instructions for escape to this believing and expectant crowd are simply to raise their heads and look up as these signs begin to appear—for their Salvation draws near. They will be long gone before the dread fully develops, long before the abomination of desolation stands in the Holy Place as prophesied by Daniel and Jesus (let the reader understand).

They are not to run nor flee nor fight for their *Lord is coming* for them as He promised so many times when He was here. *This is no Dream. It is* the *Word of God*

These two very different audiences are also powerfully evident in the Two presentations of the coming of the Lord and in the parables of the trees with which Jesus concludes. Refer to the tables of *The Analysis* for this development.

The notes and arrangement of *The Analysis* were designed to tie Matthew's and Luke's series of events and their common end time signs to their fulfillment in history past, and in the history yet to come. The prophecy-confirming history of the early church is taken from The New Testament and that of 70 AD is taken from Josephus. This present generation continues to be the eyewitness of prophecy-confirming modern history.

No commentaries were consulted in preparing this table, only the Scriptures and histories, notably Josephus. While this table and this introduction are far from complete and, without doubt, contain errors and inaccuracies they have been held in preparation for far too long already. They are submitted at this very late date for your prayerful consideration, correction, and completion. Go with God. The time is short

Dear reader, let me say by way of encouragement to you, that it is recognized that *The Analysis* tables are perhaps the most difficult part of this story to read simply because they are not, on the surface, in a narrative form. However, the narrative is there. It is just in a very condensed form. It is in an outline for sake of brevity. Read it very carefully and let God's Spirit guide you in fleshing out the story at your own pace. It contains the underlying basis of all that has been set forth so far, and far more. Expect to read it many times before it surrenders all of its value.

Consider your study of *The Analysis* tables, as similar to that part of an adventure story where the famous explorer-archeologist kneels down in the light of a flickering torch to decipher a lost language text engraved on the lid of a dusty sarcophagus in the heart of an ancient pyramid filled with deadly traps and many skeletons. Only, instead of just reading fiction about it, you have the honor of doing it, nonfiction, in your own real life. Don't flag; press on as if your life depended on it. It very well may. You see there are still deadly traps and many skeletons lurking near by.

As you will see, the main format of the tables is a four-column spread with abbreviated and truncated texts of Matthew 24 and Luke 21 NKJV occupying the two center columns. The flanking columns contain running comments on these texts. Consult your Bible or the previous section, *The Scriptures*, for the full texts of these chapters.

The best way to get the most out of this presentation is to proceed down the page line by line, first comparing The Scriptures which lie side-by-side, then comparing the comments on The Scriptures that flank them and then returning to the texts again. Don't try to absorb the whole page at once, any more than you would try to absorb this page at once. But even as you read this page line by line, read *The Analysis* line by line, even covering the rest of the page with a blank sheet of paper, if necessary to maintain the focus. Please read the titles, subtitles and all headings for they will help to organize the presentation in your mind. Again, God's Speed.

The Analysis

Matthew 24		Luke 21		
Notes	**Abbreviated Text**	**Abbreviated Text**	**Notes**	
Jesus' Declaration				
	2 Not one stone shall be left here upon another that shall not be thrown down	**6** The days will come in which not one stone shall be left upon another that shall not be thrown down.		
The Disciples' Questions				
Two questions: *When* will The Temple Stones come down? *What will be the sign* of Your coming and the End of the Age? These are end time questions. The Tribulation Jews & other Tribulation Time Saints will need the encouragement of Jesus' answer to these questions to sustain their faith in a time yet to come.	**3** When will all this be? What will be the signs of *Your Coming* and of the *End Of The Age?*	**7** When will these things be and what sign will there be when these things are about to take place?	Two questions, dealing only with Herod's Temple: *When* will the Temple stones be thrown down? *What sign* will precede this? No questions are asked about the end of the age or His return. Only Luke records that part of Jesus' answers that deals with these two specific near term questions.	

77

Matthew 24		Luke 21	
Jesus' Response			
Notes	**Abbreviated Text**	**Abbreviated Text**	**Notes**
Verse 4 gives the *only warning against* being deceived in Matthew's account. There are also *three* notifications *that deception will occur* delivered in Matthew in verses 5, 11, and 24. Jesus then tells them of the false christs and false signs which, must be distinguished from the *true signs* which follow.	**4, 5, 6** Take heed that no one deceives you. False christs will come and *will deceive many.* You will hear of wars and rumors of war. See that you are not troubled. For all these things must come to pass, *but the end is not yet.*	**8, 9** Take heed that you not be deceived. For many will come in my name, saying I am He and the time draws near. Therefore do not go after them but when you hear of wars and commotions, do not be terrified for these things must come to pass first, *but the end will not come immediately.*	This is the *first and last* time that Jesus warns Luke's audience *not to be deceived.* When Matthew's audience is notified that many will be deceived *on two more occasions* in Matthew verses 11 and 24 Luke's audience isn't on earth. Luke then tells them of the false christs and false signs, which must be distinguished from the *true signs* which follow. The wars and commotions are all of history's convulsions which come before the signs of the final days.

Matthew 24		Luke 21	
Notes	Abbreviated Text	Abbreviated Text	Notes
Jesus Now Gives The True Signs of the beginning of the end. Only the first *five signs* are listed here as the beginning of sorrows (see vs. 8). *The sixth sign* is first given in verse 29 at the very end of the Great Tribulation as the final herald of Jesus' return and the end of the age. All of the events recorded in Matthew occur during The Tribulation, between the first five beginning signs and the final sixth sign. *Matthew 24 tells us almost nothing of world history before the signs begin.*	**7** 1. Nation will rise against nation 2. Kingdom against kingdom 3. Famines 4. Pestilence 5. Earthquakes	**10, 11** 1. Nation against nation 2. Kingdom against kingdom 3. Earthquakes 4. Famines 5. Pestilence 6. *Fearful Sights and great signs from heaven.*	*The True Signs* of the end. *All six signs* are listed here. *The sixth sign* is also repeated in verse 26 (to close the parenthesis on the verses 12-24 prelude). As you will see in verse 12, all of these signs are preceded by the events recorded in verses 12-24 which tells us that these signs will not begin until the whole sequence of the following described events is finished. *Luke tells us nothing of what transpires during The Tribulation, which occurs between the first five signs and the sixth sign.*

Matthew 24		Luke 21	
Notes	**Abbreviated Text**	**Abbreviated Text**	**Notes**
These 5 signs of verse 7 are the *first part* of the sorrows. The 6th isn't. It concludes The Tribulation. (vs. 29)	**8** All of these things are the *beginning* of sorrows.	There is no equivalent foreboding warning in Luke.	Because Luke is written to those who will not experience the sorrows and don't need the warning.
According to the *"Then" of vs. 9,* all of The Tribulation events, *which follow in the text,* including the sign of the abomination of desolation standing in the Holy Place, which is the sign to flee to the mountains, *must follow after the signs of verse 7.*	**9 Then** they will deliver you up to *tribulation:* • Kill you • You will be hated by all nations **10** Will betray and hate one another	**12** *But, before all these things:* • They will lay hands on you • And persecute you • Delivering to synagogues and prisons • You will be brought before kings and rulers.	The *"But before all these things" of verse 12 declares that the events from this verse through verse 24 happen before the signs of verses 10 & 11 begin.* these events, which must come first, include, not only the early persecutions of the church, but also: • the sign of the surrounding armies which precedes the desolation of Jerusalem and the warning to flee to the mountains;

Matthew 24		Luke 21	
Notes	Abbreviated Text	Abbreviated Text	Notes
Verse 11 includes the second notification in Matthew of the deception of many. *Again all of these events follow chronologically after the first five signs. (But before the sixth sign.)* In fact, everything that Jesus describes all of the way to verse 29 will happen between the 5 signs of verse 7 and the 6th sign of verse 29.	11 False prophets will arise and deceive many. 12 Lawless will abound and love will grow cold. 13 But *he who endures to the end will be saved.* 14 And this gospel of the kingdom will be preached in all the world as a witness to all nations. • *And then the end will come.*	16 Betrayed by family and friends; • put some of you to death 17 Hated 18 *But not a hair of your head shall be lost.* 19 By your patience possess your souls.	• the overthrow of the city and the leading off of the people into captivity; • and the trampling of Jerusalem under foot by the Gentiles *until the time of the Gentiles is fulfilled.* *All of these events must occur before any of the six signs of verses 10 &11 can even begin.*

Matthew 24

Notes	Abbreviated Text
15 Antiochus IV Epiphanies pre filled this sign (also mentioned *four times* in Daniel) in 168 BC, many years before Jesus reinstated it in this prophesy. A review of its first fulfillment by the Greeks is instructive in understanding its ultimate fulfillment. That is why the Spirit instructs Matthew to add, "Let the reader understand." This sign played no part in the destruction of Jerusalem in 70 AD. The Romans held the Temple in great awe. They did not defile it. It was set on fire after the city was surrounded and its defenses breached, which was not a useful sign for escape.	**15** When you see the abomination of desolation spoken of by Daniel standing in the holy place (let the reader understand.)

Luke 21

Abbreviated Text	Notes
20 When you see Jerusalem surrounded by armies know that its desolation is near.	**20** In 70 AD Vespasian stationed Roman units around Jerusalem after reducing all of the rest of the Jewish cities, but news of Nero's death caused him to delay the final siege and gave those inside the city who knew and trusted Jesus' words an opportunity to escape. Vespasian later sent his son, Titus, to complete the reduction of the city. This desolation of Jerusalem is a well-documented historical fact. So are all of the other events foretold in order from Verse 12 through and including the last part of Verse 24. The Gentiles did trample Jerusalem under foot until June 1967.

Matthew 24		Luke 21	
Notes	**Abbreviated Text**	**Abbreviated Text**	**Notes**
16-20 The escalation of terror and horror that occurs in the middle of The Tribulation when the Antichrist desecrates the Temple and declares that he is God occurs as suddenly as the closure of the Roman Army siege circle around Rome in 70 AD. (Let the reader understand). These warnings and instructions are for the last escape that Jesus addresses. Dear Believer, Dear Tribulation Saint, if you are still here, don't miss it, because what is coming next is the worst of all times.	**16** Let those who are in Judea flee to the mountains. **17** Let him who is on the housetop not go down to take anything out of his house. **18** And let him who is in the field not go back to get his clothes. **19** But woe to those who are pregnant and to those who are nursing babies in those days! **20** And pray that your flight may not be in winter or on the sabbath.	**21** Let those who are in Judea flee to the mountains, let those who are in the midst of her depart, and let those who are in the country not enter her. **22** For these are the days of vengeance, that all things that are written may be fulfilled. **23** But woe to those who are pregnant and to those who are nursing babies in those days! for there will be *great distress in the land and wrath upon this people.*	**21** The first century believers who followed Jesus' instructions escaped the destruction of the City in the summer of 70 AD. **22** As Jesus also prophesied with such vehemence in Matthew 23:34-38. **23** The Distress and Wrath of 70 AD was limited to *The Land* and *This People* as this prophecy of Jesus of those days clearly specified. It was not on the same scale as the almost unlimited and unspecified terror of the End of Days Tribulation foretold by Jesus in Matthew 24:21.

Matthew 24		Luke 21	
Notes	**Abbreviated Text**	**Abbreviated Text**	**Notes**
21 This Great Tribulation, following the Temple's desecration, by God's own definition hasn't happened yet. Not in 70 AD. Not in the Holocaust. This worst of all times is yet to be. It is the end of the age as also spoken of by Daniel (*Daniel 12:1b, "And there shall be a time of trouble, Such as never was since there was a nation, even to that time And at that time your people shall be delivered, Every one that is found written in the book."*)	**21** For there will then be *Great Tribulation* such as has not been since the beginning of the world until this time, *No, nor ever shall be.*	**24** And they will fall by the edge of the sword and be lead away captive into all nations and Jerusalem will be trampled by the Gentiles. *Until the times of the Gentiles are fulfilled.*	**24** The last half of this verse having been fulfilled in 1967, all of the events that Jesus says must come before the final signs that precede the Temple's final desecration, His Coming and the End of the Age have all been completed, and in our own generation. The beginning of the signs of verses 10 & 11 can now actually be anticipated in reality. *For the first time in history the rapture is actually imminent.* Not only has Jerusalem been liberated, but also around the world, the Japhetic Gentile tribes have reached their zenith.

Matthew 24		Luke 21	
Notes	**Abbreviated Text**	**Abbreviated Text**	**Notes**
22 "Elect" refers, in the first instance, to the Jewish Remnant (See Romans 11 as a good example). Matthew uses it. Luke does not. (Dan 12:7, The Man in white linen --swore that -- when the power of the holy people has been completely shattered, all these things shall be finished.)	**22** Unless those days were shortened *no flesh* would be saved, but for the elect's sake those days will be shortened.	**22** In Luke There Is Nothing Like Matthew's Verse 22.	**22** Luke's believers will *not be on earth* during this time of intense and wide spread slaughter, *neither will they be in the flesh.* Matthew's words are not for them. These elect will have already been rescued by Jesus.
23 This is the *third* warning of false christs/prophets in Matthew. *For the first time, however, the reader is warned that these false ones will be given the power to show great signs and wonders. The Final Antichrist and his cohorts! See II Thessalonians Chapter 2 for total confirmation of this fact in almost exactly these same words.*	**23** False christs and false prophets showing great signs & wonders to deceive the very *elect* if possible.	**23** No equivalent warning of such a threat to faith is found in Luke.	**23** No warning necessary because Luke's "elect" will have already escaped from this earthly realm where deception dwells long before this fearful time arrives. Matthew's audience has been told *twice before that many will be deceived.* Luke's believers have been *warned once not to be deceived.* Those in whom the Holy Spirit dwells only require admonition. Those of the world will be deceived regardless of the number of warnings.

Matthew 24

Notes	Abbreviated Text
29 The sixth sign is now finally given as occurring at the end of The Tribulation as the sign of the immediacy of His Coming and the End of the Age.	**29** Immediately after the **Tribulation** of those days – signs in sun, moon, stars & *powers of heaven will be shaken.*

Luke 21

Abbreviated Text	Notes
25 There will be signs in sun, moon, stars and **26** Men's hearts failing because of fear; *Powers of heaven will be shaken.*	**25 & 26** The sixth sign is repeated and amplified signifying that Luke's *"But before all these things"* prelude of verses 12 through 24 has now ended. The telling now proceeds in chronological order. From this point on Matthew and Luke are synchronous, however, they address the same two different audiences as before, those who listen early and those who listen late.

Matthew 24

Notes

30 The *seventh* sign of the Son of Man will then appear and no one will be able to deny His identity. Then all of the tribes of the earth (*they*, not *we*) will mourn and *they* will see Him but not as Savior except for the elect remnant who have believed and endured The Tribulation, faithful to the end, obtaining their salvation. Perhaps, even the elect will mourn with heart broken grief for what they have done and for what they have suffered when they see the one whom they pierced.

The seventh sign is described by Jesus in *Matthew 26:64*.

Abbreviated Text

30 Then the sign of the Son of Man will appear in heaven and all of the tribes of the earth will mourn and they will see the Son of Man coming with power and great glory.

Luke 21

Abbreviated Text

27 Then *"they"* will see the Son of Man coming in a cloud with power and great glory.

Notes

27 *This is the same "they" as in Matthew, the mourning lost and* the surviving tribulation Saints, all of the tribes still on earth, Luke's Raptured early believers will not be among *their* number.

Matthew 24		Luke 21	
Notes	**Abbreviated Text**	**Abbreviated Text**	**Notes**
At His trial Jesus answered His accusers when they charged Him with claiming to be the Son of God. Jesus said, "It is as you said, nevertheless, I say to you, hereafter you will see the *Son of Man sitting at the right hand of the Power, and coming on the clouds of heaven.*" At the end of the last days the clouds will be rolled back and even His accusers will be shown a view right into heaven to see Him seated at God's right hand just before He comes, a sure sign of His authority and their condemnation and impending doom.	*Matthew is ominously silent.* This promise of redemption, this beacon of hope of *Luke 21:28* is not reported in Matthew's account at all.	**28** Now when *these things begin to happen,* look up and lift up your head because your redemption draws near.	**28** But those of us who heed these warning words of Jesus in Luke and discern the *very beginning* of *"these things,"* which are the first five signs of vs. 10 & 11 there is cause for hope and indeed, *rejoicing,* not mourning as the lost will mourn, because our *redemption* draws near when these things begin to happen at the very dawning of the first five signs which are the beginning of sorrows, long before the sixth, much less the seventh sign appear.

Matthew 24		Luke 21	
Notes	Abbreviated Text	Abbreviated Text	Notes
There is no early escape for Matthew's readers. By the time these slow believers read this account this escape opportunity will have passed. They will have to die a martyr's death or endure to the very bitter end in order to inherit eternal life. Read The Revelation for more details on what they will face and what those who eagerly wait for their Lord's return will miss because as He promised He will catch them up from the face of the earth to be with Him forever. *This is no dream.* This is His promise			When these things begin to happen there is to be no fleeing to the mountains to escape tribulation, rather we are to stay in our place, look up, lift our heads and behold the salvation of the Lord.

Matthew 24		Luke 21	
Notes	**Abbreviated Text**	**Abbreviated Text**	**Notes**
31 The Elect, the surviving Jews and all others who have endured the Great Tribulation faithful to the end from all over the earth will now be gathered to their Lord.	**31** And He will send His angels with great trumpet sound to gather the elect from the four winds, from one end of heaven to the other.	The account of this gathering recorded in *Matthew 24:31 is missing* from Luke.	This account is missing because that portion of the elect that Luke is addressing will have already been gathered to Him at that earlier trumpet sound which will call the early faithful to rise to Him in the clouds on the day of rapture, preceded only by Jesus and those who are asleep in Jesus on that day. *I Thessalonians 4:13-18* and *I Corinthians 15:22-26, 35-58* Confirm this.

Matthew 24	*Luke 21*		
Postlude: The Parable of the Fig Tree (and other trees)			
In this parable Jesus teaches that the *birth pains*, *the five beginning signs*, are the harbingers of the *final days*. He teaches that we must intensely examine world events to discern their approach so that we might be ready for the season they foretell. The parable carries this message at two levels.			
Notes	**Abbreviated Text**	**Abbreviated Text**	**Notes**
32 "The fig tree". The Jews to whom Matthew wrote knew fig trees, in fact the prophets often likened the Jewish nation to figs, usually over ripe figs. Since, indeed, the Jewish nation is sometimes likened to figs, maybe the flowering of Israel in our day is the sign of the fig tree putting forth leaves, that Jesus was talking about. Summer is near.	**32** Now learn this parable from the fig tree: When its branch has already become tender and puts forth leaves, you know that summer is near.	**29** Then he spoke to them a parable. Look at the fig tree and all the trees. **30** When they are already budding, you see and know for yourselves that summer is now near.	**29 & 30** "And all the trees." The message carried by Luke is to all the Gentile world, including climes where the fig tree is not known. So the parable is understandable, even if one doesn't know the seasons of the fig tree. Also in our day, battling old world Kingdom empires flay at one another and give Nations long suppressed by them the opportunities to bud on their own. Such are the OPEC Nations, the young tigers of Asia, the newly freed republics of Eastern Europe and the old USSR, the striving tribes of Africa and the ethnic uprisings in the islands of the sea. All the trees are budding, Summer is near.

It is Coming

Matthew 24

Notes	Abbreviated Text
33 "*All* these things" are the signs that Jesus gave the apostles and The Tribulation events that He foretold. Matthew's primary audience will experience "*all* these things" before His coming and the End of the Age and those who endure in faith to the end will be saved. The "it" is the end of the age and the return of our Lord.	**33** So you also, when you see *all* these things know that *it* is near—even at the door!

Luke 21

Abbreviated Text	Notes
31 So you also, when you see these things *happening*, know that the *Kingdom of God* is near.	**31** "These Things" are the signs that Jesus gave the apostles As verse 28 says, "when *these things begin* to happen, look up and lift up your head because your redemption draws near". Verse 31 has the same import. "When you see these things happening" doesn't require that all actions be complete, just recognizably begun. For the ready believers, the beginning of the signs herald the *Kingdom of God* and *Redemption*, not judgment, not mourning.

92

Matthew 24		Luke 21	
Notes	**Abbreviated Text**	**Abbreviated Text**	**Notes**
34 & 35 "This generation" is the one that sees the signs and experiences the events to which Jesus has just referred. Fulfillment will be in their lifetime. Jesus strongly confirms His own words just as God confirmed His Promise to Abraham by an oath (Heb 6:17); and the Man in White Linen over the waters in Daniel 12:7 confirmed His word by oath. *The earth will pass away but Jesus' confirmed words will not pass away.* Jesus' Confirmed Words are: *"This Generation will not pass away until all these things take place".*	**34** Assuredly I say to you *this* generation *will by no means pass away* till all these things take place. **35** Heaven and earth *will pass away,* but my words will *by no means pass away.*	**32** Assuredly, I say to you *this* generation *will by no means pass away* till all things take place. **33** Heaven and earth *will pass away, but my words will by no means pass away.*	**32 & 33** For the *only* time in these chapters these verses in Luke are *essentially identical* to the corresponding verses (34 & 35) in Matthew and (30 & 31) in Mark. This unique triple repetition seals Jesus' oath. (See the final table, *Jesus' promise to the last generation,* for a more detailed treatment of these vital verses). *"This generation"* is the generation that sees the signs that Jesus just gave and experiences the end time events that follow. Fulfillment is in their lifetime. It is going to happen and on the timetable Jesus has just set out. We have Jesus' confirmed word on it. That you can trust!

In addition to the "Assuredly" with which Jesus begins this declaration, the three-fold repetition of the words "pass away", twice confirming, once denying, tie these three declarations of Jesus together into the single strongest divine oath found in all Scripture. For final shouting impact this oath is uniquely repeated with the exact same meaning three times over in the Scriptures, being in all three accounts: Matthew, Mark and Luke. This is not just poetry!

Matthew 24

Notes	Abbreviated Text
There is no equivalent warning in Matthew to Luke's 34. Matthew's tardy readers are not even looking for him!	*Matthew is ominously silent.* Because by the time his audience reads this text, this day of escape will have already passed them by.

Luke 21

Abbreviated Text	Notes
34 But take heed to yourselves, lest your hearts be weighed down with carousing, drunkenness, and cares of this life, and that day come on you unexpectedly.	**34** Remember Verse 28: "Now when *these things begin to happen,* look up and lift up your head because your *redemption draws near*". This *day of redemption* is the day of escape for the redeemed. Those eagerly expecting to join Him in the air do not know the day or hour, but they will not be surprised by His arrival, His call and their escape unless they let themselves become weighed down by current events or escapist dissipation.

Matthew 24

Notes	Abbreviated Text
Matthew's silence is indeed dreadful. Those who are not caught up on that day at the beginning will be left caught in the snare of their unchanged bodies upon the face of the earth to be engulfed in the coming holocaust.	*Again, Matthew is ominously silent.*

Luke 21

Abbreviated Text	Notes
35 For it will come as a snare on all those who dwell on the face of the whole earth.	**35** It will surprise all those not eagerly desiring and expecting Him. His coming will be a snare for all those who dwell on the face of the whole earth, for His coming will seal their fate. Only those who rise to meet Jesus in the air on *that day* of escape at the very beginning of The Tribulation will escape from the face of the earth where all who will be saved must then either die a martyr's death or endure the great tribulation faithful to the very end.

Matthew 24

Notes	Abbreviated Text
No means of escape from the great tribulation is offered to Matthew's readers. However, those who endure, persevering faithful to the end will be saved. This will be their precious encouragement in the time of their great distress.	Again, Matthew is ominously silent.

Luke 21

Abbreviated Text	Notes
36 Watch therefore, and pray always that you may be counted worthy to escape all these things that will come to pass, and to stand before the Son of Man.	**36** Eagerly watch (for the beginning of the signs and His appearance) and pray for steadfastness of faith in the face of temptation in anticipation of your escape from the great tribulation that will come to all those caught on the face of the earth. Pray that instead of being caught on earth during The Tribulation that you will instead *be standing redeemed in the heavens before the Son of Man* while these dreadful things happen to all who dwell on the face of the earth during the final purging and reaping of this present age.

Let the *Lord* bless you as you meditate on the following *Scriptures* as you prepare your heart for *His harvest.*

John 14: 1-3	I Thessalonians 5:23	I Thessalonians 1:10	II Thessalonians 2
I Thessalonians 3:12 & 13	Daniel 12	Philippians 3: 20 & 21	Hebrews 9:28
Colossians 3:4	II Timothy 4: 8	II Thessalonians 3: 12 & 13	Titus 2:11-13
Zechariah 11-14	Revelation	I Corinthians 1: 7 & 8	Isaiah 9:6-7

"Now when these things begin to happen, look up and lift up your head because your redemption draws near"

The Promise

Jesus' promise to the last generation

In *Jesus'* discourse *He* tells of the terrible events of the final days, the means of escaping or surviving them and the signs that will immediately precede them. This relationship between signs, events and escapes was, after all, the central issue of His disciple's questions. To relate the timing of the signs to the events they portend and to the escapes He uses expressions like, "when you see these things happening, or beginning to happen, take notice that the time of the end is near".

To illustrate this relationship Jesus then gives the parable of the trees putting forth buds as a sign that summer is near. He says that when you see these botanical signs you know that summer is near and in like manner when you see the signs I have just given you, you know that the time of the end is near. How near? *At the door.* He says that this very generation shall not pass away until all these things have been fulfilled. The generation that He has just identified as the one that first sees the signs will not pass away until all is fulfilled. He is saying that when you see these signs, you are on notice that you are the final generation. Everything will be completed before your generation passes away. It is this final generation that He is warning to take heed to the signs of the end, even to the very faint beginnings of these signs. He wants the last generation to know that it is the last generation

In this oath He declares that the fact that the generation that first sees the signs is also the final generation is as immutable as His very words. *He* seals this, His *warning* and *His promise* to *the last generation* with an *oath*. This is His oath. The endurance of His everlasting words is the standard by which we are to judge the endurance of the final generation. Do His words endure? Even so shall the final witnessing generation endure until the very end.

These everlasting words He is referring to are specifically the words of this prophecy. Indeed, the completely accurate fulfillment of the whole of His prophecy given on the Mount of Olives so far, to this late date, is further confirmation, as if God's word needed any confirmation at all, that His Word does, in fact, endure, undiminished throughout the ages. His recently fulfilled prophecy of the Jew's return to Jerusalem after nearly two thousand years, and this, in this, our very own generation, is proof enough of that. What further proof do you seek? If you wait until He is revealed in heaven in glory to believe, that will be sight, not faith, and it will be too late. Then the whole world will believe, but it will be too late. Now is the time to choose sides. We are saved by faith, not by sight!

We surely know that God's Word endures forever. We now know that Jesus is God, because His Words also endure as He claimed they would. And He is generous enough to our weak and wavering faith to give us proof of that, one more time in our own late generation: the fulfillment of His own prophetic word.

Praise him! He has come with us to the end of the age.

Indeed all of the Words of God are imperishable and will never fade away as these verses proclaim. Christians of all persuasions take great comfort in these passages and apply them to all the promises of God, as they should. But should they not be applied directly, with the greatest force and faith, to the very promise to which Jesus, Himself, applied them? Yes, and what is that promise? That promise is that the generation that sees the signs and events, which He says will herald the end of this era, will not pass away until all the things of this era are completed. The culmination of all things, from the very beginnings of the signs until His return in glory, will not take place over centuries, not over generations, *but in a single lifetime! Most likely, ours!*

What an encouragement to those who must endure the horrors of the final days! These days will not last forever.

What a wake up call to those who long for and expect His imminent return and their escape from the horrors of these last days! He is at the door ready to take them up and out when these signs begin.

This last table, *"Jesus' Promise to the Last Generation"* is a study of God's declaration and confirming oath for completing His dealings with man. Although fore-figured by the awesome oath recorded in *Daniel 12:7*, this, His promise, His warning and His oath concerning the final generation which is found in triplicate in *Matthew 24 verses 34 and 35*, *Mark 13 verses 30* and *31* and *Luke 21 verses 32 and 33* is unique in all *Scripture* for the power of its expression of the divine will and order.

It is no coincidence, and of compelling interest, that both of these extraordinary oath-bound declarations which are found in Daniel and in triplicate in these Gospel Accounts are uttered specifically to confirm the *time limits* that God, *Himself*, has placed on His dealings with His creation during the final terrible days that occur at the culmination of this age. Why is this? Does He really want us to know the times and seasons? Is it that important to Him? Ponder this in your heart. He uses all of His power of expression to tell the final generation that it is the final generation and that time is up. He sets the limits of creation and time, beginning and end.

He is the setter of dates, Author and Finisher, Alpha and Omega, the Initiator and Ender of all things.

It is evident, against all arguments, that the three accounts of Jesus' Mount of Olive Discourse are all quite different and for very good reasons as has been set forth. It is also equally evident that the three records are essentially identical when it comes to reporting this oath of promise and warning uttered by Jesus. The verses that record this oath are the *only* verses in all of the discourse that bear this unique identity in all three of the records. The oath is in triplicate. It is a triune oath. No other words of His in all of His teachings in all of the Gospels exceed the force of this expression of His will. Jesus really wants us to get the message and like its earlier edition in *Daniel 12:7 it is a message of the timing of the end. Take notice. Give heed. He wants us to know!*

This is no dream.

Study the table. Note the notes. *God* Bless

**Jesus' Promise To The Last Generation
That He Confirmed By A Triune Oath**

A study of:

	Matthew 24: 34-35		Mark 13: 30-31		Luke 21:32-33
English Equivalent	Strong's Numbers +	English Equivalent	Strong's Numbers +	English Equivalent	Strong's Numbers +
Verse 34		**Verse 30**		**Verse 32**	
Truly #	281	Truly	281	Truly	281
I say	3004	I say	3004	I say	3004
To you	5213	To you	5213	To you	5213
(No word)	(No word)	(No word)	3754	(No word)	3754
In No*	3756	In No	3756	In No	3364 = 3756
Way*	3361	Way	3361	Way	+3361
Passes Away	3928	Passes Away	3928	Passes Away	3928
Generation	1074	Generation	1074	Generation	1074
This	3778	This	3778	This	3778
Until	2193	Until	2193	Until	2193
(Not translated)	302	(Not translated)	302	(Not translated)	302
All these	3956	All these	3956	All these	3956
Things	5023	Things	5023	Things	(No word)
Have occurred	1096	Have occurred	1096	Have occurred	1096
Verse 35		**Verse 31**		**Verse 33**	
Heaven	3772	Heaven	3772	Heaven	3772
Earth	1093	Earth	1093	Earth	1093
Passes Away	3928	Passes Away	3928	Passes Away	3928
Word	3056	Word	3056	Word	3056
My	3450	My	3450	My	3450
In No	3364 = 3756+	In No	3756	In No	3364 = 3756
Way	3361	Way	3361	Way	+3361
Passes Away	3928	Passes Away	3928	Passes Away	3928

100

Table Notes

This table is derived from The Interlinear Greek–English New Testament, Second and Revised Edition, 1984, Jay P. Green, Sr., General Editor and Translator.

+ A number, from Strong's Concordance, which is uniquely assigned to each original language word in the Bible and used for cross referencing in word studies.

An analysis of what Jesus said and what He meant in this Promise Oath

 # Truly—This word is the *Amen* both in Greek and in Hebrew. When Jesus uses it to introduce a teaching, He is not just saying that this is a trust worthy saying since all of His sayings are indeed trust worthy. By invoking it, He is using all of the power that words can carry to call our attention to the vital importance *to us* of what He is saying. *We* will be judged by His words.

*In no way—The Greek words behind these words form a double negative, which, unlike the English, does not cancel out the negative meaning but, in fact, doubles the negative emphasis. Essentially, "In no way" (Strong's 3756 and 3361) is: *no! no!* or *not! not!* In verses 34, 30 & 32 Jesus, in essence, says: Truly, I say to you, this generation *shall not, shall not* pass away until all these things have occurred. This same powerful, double negative emphasis also declares His word to be eternal in verses 35, 31 and 33. This use in these later verses defines its use in the previous verses.

His enduring Words are both the Standard and the Judge.

Jesus guarantees His guarantee and then He explains it. And then the Holy Spirit repeats it three times for emphasis.

All three accounts are essentially identical only in these two verses. Here, but nowhere else. Amazing! Thus our God: confirms, confirms, confirms that this generation shall not, shall not pass away until all these things have occurred.

What more could Jesus say? What Jesus said is what He meant. This is no dream. This is not poetry. It is just plain facts to be believed, if you dare.

The Plea

An end note to our dear Jewish readers and to all others; Buddhists, Hindus, Muslims, Pagans, doubting Christians, atheists, friends, neighbors, enemies, family and foreigners who have not yet fully settled in their hearts that Jesus is the Messiah and Lord.

Think about it. There is *only One* who knows the end before the beginning. The rest of us don't even know what the next second brings. The One who knows is the Living God, Who in the beginning created all things, Who by His power sustains all things, and Who at last will call all things into account at the day He has appointed. The Living God, the I Am. Jehovah is His Name.

The Spirit by the prophet Amos said, "Surely the Lord God does nothing unless He reveals His secrets to His servants, the prophets."

Jehovah, Lord of Hosts, has sent His Prophets to His people throughout time to reveal His will to them. But He *never* revealed the circumstances of the end clearly to any of the prophets. The final chapter of the book was always shut. It was always veiled. It was always sealed until Jesus.

He further tells us through His prophet *Isaiah*, in *chapter 48 verses 5 through 8*, that He has revealed what is to be, so that when it happens, we will not attribute it to other sources or causes or claim our own special superior understanding.

Jehovah also declares in *Isaiah 46:9-10*, that *He* and *He* alone can tell *the end from the beginning.*

"For I am God, and there is none else; I am God, and there is none like Me; Declaring the end from the beginning, and from ancient times things that are not yet done."

God reserved the final clear and open declaration of *the end* to the *One* who would also be authenticated thereby as *The Great I Am*.

He says that He and He alone can tell the end from the beginning.

In the New Testament Gospel accounts of

Matthew 24 and *Luke 21*, Jesus sets forth plainly the time line of events from the beginning of the age of grace, which commenced shortly after He ascended to heaven, until His return from heaven in glory at the end of this age.

All of the events He foretold to this day have taken place *as described and in order without a single failure*, from the destruction of Jerusalem in the time of the lives of the men of His own generation, some *thirty eight years after He prophesied*, to the removal of the trampling Gentile boot from Jerusalem in this generation of our own lives *some nineteen hundred and thirty five years after He prophesied*. God said no one could foretell the end but Himself.

Jesus is the one, the only one, that has ever told the end from the beginning.

For this last generation, skeptical and far removed from the great miracles of old, God has graciously and faithfully set His witness before our very eyes at this extremity of the age by fulfilling His prophesies in our days—the Jews having been raised as dead bones out of the graveyards of the nations of their dispersion and restored to their land. The trampling boot has been removed from Jerusalem. This last event prophesied specifically and only by Jesus confirms also His claim to be the great eternal I Am, knowing and telling the end from the beginning. He was right when He said His words would endure forever. History has proved His claim. Our faith in His plain testimony on *what is yet to be* rests firmly on His prophetic record, which is perfect!

The history of the world for the last two thousand years, as it has rolled out the fulfillment of the prophecies from these two chapters alone, is *sufficient proof by itself* that Jesus is not only a trustworthy prophet but also is indeed, Lord and God. He and He alone has clearly foretold the end of the age.

Our gracious God has not left this final generation without evidence, which our own eyes can witness. He has come with us even to the end of the age just as He promised. Believe! The very few elements of His prophecy that remain unfulfilled as of this late date will also come to pass in order and on .

This is no dream. It is written in the Word.

time as all the others have, and that, most likely, in our very own generation.

If this evidence is not clear to you yet, watch carefully and pray that your eyes will be opened to see the sure hand of God, as it moves in the affairs of men and nature confirming Jesus as The Messiah, His Only Begotten Son, before summer is gone and the harvest passes and it is again, too late.

However, if this evidence that meets your eyes and your ears reaches your heart, repent and hurry and kiss the Son.

Let Him forgive you, wash you and cleanse you of your sins, immersing you in the water and by His Spirit sprinkling you with His blood, giving you a clear conscience and a clean, pure and holy heart.

So that by His grace and by His power and through His love, He can pour His Holy Spirit, which is His love, His very Own Spirit, into your heart that the Son has newly made clean and pure and holy; your heart, which He will make His Holy Temple, His abiding place; that special place on this earth where He chooses to dwell through His Spirit, so that He can live in you and you can live in Him, an overcoming life in all His great power. And whereby, on the day He calls, you can also arise and rise to meet Him in the air because He lives in you through His Spirit that He has given you.

God is Spirit. God is love.This is the gift of God that He wants to give to you now, even to pour out into your heart His own love, His own Spirit and thus even His own very Life, even Eternal Life, starting even now. He wants to do this for you, because He who made you also loves you.

He wants to do this for you so that He may live in you *this very day* and that you also may be where He is *on that very special day when He comes to receive His own*, that very special day, which is coming so very soon. Do not delay. Every knee will bow and every tongue will confess. *You will acknowledge Him.*

Acknowledge Him today with great rejoicing, great salvation or wait until it is too late and do it with great, great sorrow. You will do it sooner or later; all men will do it. Dear one, beloved of God, for whom Jesus died, kiss the Son today with great rejoicing.

Maranatha

But Before All These Things

*How the Original Story
of the End Got
Twisted and Why*

The Purpose of Part III

"But before all these things" is the first phrase of *Luke 21:12* and is an important key for unraveling long and broadly held misconceptions about the end times and, indeed, about all of world history and *about much of what Jesus taught.* That is why *Part III* of *It Is Coming* was given this title.

This Part III has the special purpose of shedding light on the huge impact of these misconceptions on history and on today's traditions, culture, mindset, thought-patterns, values, and current events.

Part III also attempts to trace a particular line of the dark and twisted strain of rebellion and disbelief in the human heart down through the ages. It attempts to gain a glimpse of those forces which have sustained an artful campaign of disinformation on vital issues impacted by this phrase and the associated teachings of Jesus. It attempts to shed light on this campaign of deception which has helped bring the world and the worldly church to its present very dangerous and ungodly condition.

Tracing these things out, as best we are able, should help us to better understand the historical setting of our situation today. This understanding should bolster *our faith* as we face today's challenges, *our precious faith*, so utterly essential for our participation in His wonderful plans for us *to escape* all of that, which is about to fall on all of those who will soon be trapped here below on earth.

Warning! This *Part III* contains some subject matter that may well be nothing more substantial than an editorial opinion. Approach it with care and bear your own responsibility. This whole section came close to being struck. Perhaps it should have been.

But remember this: *That Luke 21:12 is The Word Of God. In this you must also bear your own responsibility, and you will give your own account to the Lord.* Do not neglect the messages that cascade down from it in all directions from that day until this day and to the End of the Age, and do not neglect their ramifications for your life.

The Purpose of Part I

Part I, The Astounding Anomaly of the Gospels was written to capture your attention, as mine was, and to focus it on what Jesus really said about the End of the Age and the vitally important fact that He said it clearly and unequivocally. The uncompromising clarity of the story as He foretold it is of utmost importance *because it establishes Jesus as the One who declares the end from the beginning. God alone can do this according to Isaiah 46:9–10, and Jesus did it.*

If clearly presented to the doubters of this present age, *fulfilled* prophecy is the most conclusive proof available today of Jesus' divinity and the authenticity of the Scriptures. It is objective and external, and it is subject to impartial evaluation and independent verification. If it is clearly presented as it was clearly spoken, it is not even subject to interpretation once it has been fulfilled.

The Purpose of Part II

Part II, The View from the Mountain, is a simple presentation of the facts, in order, as presented by *Jesus on the Mount of Olives* as recorded in *Matthew 24, Mark 13* and *Luke 21*.

What Part II Does Not Address

However, *The View from the Mountain* does not directly address in any depth the damage done to the human race by the confusion which has resulted through the centuries from the traditional orthodoxy of twisting and braiding these *Scriptures* into mutual conformity.

The rationale of many expositors for maintaining this *braiding of the Scriptures* undoubtedly arose from their hypothesis that the three separate accounts were *attempting* to record *Jesus' prophecy* of the same single set of events. This forcing of accounts was viewed as the minimum effort necessary to maintain the integrity of *God's Word* by *helping* the *Prophets* keep their stories straight. The true motivation of the ultimate author of this deception lies far deeper and is much more sinister. Unveiling this deeper deception is a mission of *Part III*.

Perhaps it could be imagined that the end product, the homogenized Gospel, was simply developed to satisfy man's sense of order and reasonableness. However, even such simple hearted harmonizing, which, in

"Our warfare is against the wiles of the devil...it is not against flesh and blood, but against principalities, against powers, against the rulers of the darkness of this age, against spiritual hosts of wickedness in heavenly places." *Ephesians 6.*

this case, turns out to be the actual *censorship* of the *Scriptures,* is nothing less than attempting to challenge *God* with nothing more than human experience and human reasoning. This was *Job's* folly when he questioned God. This has always been man's greatest temptation and folly when he finally confronts God in his life. Are we to live our own life, as if God is not God, as if He does not know, does not care or maybe doesn't even exist? Or do we surrender our will to Him because He is God and we know it?

Please recognize that although many very strong, forceful sayings are found in what follows, none are directed against any human being either living or dead. The poor souls, who have been most deeply involved in these deceptions through the ages and today, deserve the deepest compassion because they, themselves, have been most deceived by the common adversary. The *Only One* who has never been deceived has the right and the standing to judge them. No one else does. The rest of us can only extend to them His compassion and His light as He gives us understanding and opportunity to do so, considering at all times our own weakness, vulnerabilities and sins.

No, it is not against them whom we come, but their captor and our common foe. *Our warfare is not against flesh and blood, but... against spiritual hosts of wickedness in heavenly places.* Those who are caught in this web of deception and yet live, we deeply love you and pray for your deliverance from our mutual adversary. These admonitions are presented with force so that the warnings will have the impact on your heart that they, and you, both deserve. It would be a total and shameful disservice to you to mince words at this late date on these matters of such vital concern. Please don't be offended, rather please think it through and pray for all of us.

Finally, please don't judge me either, *but please correct me.* For I am sure that I have not yet nearly escaped all of the deceptions of our adversary. Now let's get started on what the adversary has done to us through the centuries by means of this particular set of deceptions.

So What? Does Jesus Really Care?

The View from the Mountain does not address the possibility of dark forces and hideous purposes that may lie behind these deceptions. *But Before All These Things* does address these possibilities. As it does, it will also address the unbelievable question of: *"So what?"*

You see, after reading early drafts of *The View from the Mountain*, not withstanding the incalculable impact of the clear pronouncements of Jesus on the final generation, some actually said, *"So What?"* They said this, as if *knowing* what is coming upon the world very shortly is of no appreciable value or consequence!

They were also apparently unaware of the possibility that they, themselves, are in the cross hairs of a conspiracy that has been active these many years to obscure and even, if it were possible, *to prevent* what is coming. This "So what?" mind-set may be the very best indicator of just how successful the multi-millenial campaign of this conspiracy has been. *Some* of those who asked *"So what?"* may even believe that the end of this age is near and that the rapture could occur at any time: theoretically!

They may have worked their way to this understanding through other more difficult Scriptures and disputed passages (Or simply as blind followers of a "newer" tradition). Many of these disputed passages are, themselves, made clear by *Luke 21:12* as this verse clears up the chronology of Olivet. These believers have not recognized this to be one of the clearest of all of the statements of Jesus about the events of *the End of the Age* and *His Return* and the timing of these events and the sequence of their occurrence, including, especially, *the rapture*. They too, may be caught in the web of tradition and don't even know it.

Although they believe, they have deprived themselves of one of the clearest possible evidences available and one of the simplest means of explaining it to others.

> They too, may be caught in the web of tradition and don't even know it.

More importantly, they have also deprived themselves of the clearest evidence for themselves and especially for others in these last days of *the Divinity of Jesus*.

They may have also deprived themselves of a certain spectacular view of the big picture brought by these *chapters* of *God's eternal plan* for His people and of the adversary's age-long attack on the whole human race. They have certainly missed this evidence of the scope, the intensity and *the reality* of this great age-long battle royal that has raged without truce in heaven and on earth for millennia between the prince of this earth and the Prince of Peace.

The linkage of the *three hidden chapters of Romans* (more on this later) to this verse and the linked theft by the Worldly Christian Church of the Jewish promises and the destruction that this has wrought on mankind may have also been obscured by their failure to appreciate the weight of this plain and simple teaching of Jesus, delivered in His last week in the flesh on this earth.

They may have also deprived many others—Jews, Muslims and especially Christians of the a millenial persuasion, *who are very close and dear to them*, of an understanding of *the sure place of Israel and Jerusalem in God's closing act.*

Many of these, especially of *their dearly beloved a millenial brothers*, don't even really believe that there is a closing act or that God is still directing the play, certainly not in any time-frame that practically affects them. At least that is what I remember of my own belief in my own a millenial days.

Ironically, most of these a millenial brothers in fact, believe that God hears and answers their prayers and will heal and protect them from all harm. They believe that He knows them and cares for them. They have faith. They believe He is coming back eventually and will save them eternally. I know, I have been there. And all of this is true, if they trust Him.

But *some* of *these dearly beloved* do not really believe that He directs the *affairs of nations* in accordance with His own will and plan, that He always has and always will. In these matters they don't have faith. Maybe they don't believe Him, just because they don't understand Him. They don't understand Him, in these particular matters, mainly because the impact of *Luke 21:12* and related Scriptures has not dawned on them yet.

They believe that although He follows the flight and fall of every sparrow and hears the silent earnest plea of every heart that seeks Him, He still remains indifferent to the times, places and events of the nations and even of the entire race of men that dwell on the whole face of the earth. They don't think He has a thing to say about history after 70 AD, *especially about recent and future history.*

They really believe this about God in spite of His own testimony repeatedly declared throughout both the Old and New Testaments that He not only cares about, but He, in fact, directs the affairs of nations, sets their boundaries and their times individually, and *He sets the time for the whole human race as well,* and the end of that time is now drawing near.

Please direct *these dearly beloved* to just ten examples of God's testimony that He is in charge, calls the shots, has the clock and keeps the time, directs the affairs and blows the whistle on the nations, individually, and on the whole of the human race as well.

Here are ten examples that tell us His Heart and Mind, Plan and Will on this issue of extreme importance to this eleventh hour generation. They could be multiplied many times over, but here they are:

- *This decision is by the decree of the watchers, and the sentence by the word of the holy ones, in order for the living to know that the Most High rules in the kingdom of men, gives it to whomever He will, and sets over it the lowest of men. Daniel 4:17.* He rules in the affairs of men.
- *Who says of Cyrus, "He is my shepherd, and he shall perform all my pleasure" saying to Jerusalem, "You shall be built", and to the Temple, "your foundation shall be laid"." Isaiah 44:28.* God calls Cyrus by name 150 years before he was born!
- *And He has made from one blood every nation of men to dwell on all the face of the earth, and has determined their preappointed times and the boundaries of their dwellings so that they should seek the Lord, in the hope that they might grope for Him and find Him, though He is not far from each one of us...Acts 17:26 & 27.* Preappointed times!!!
- *Thus says the Lord, who gives the sun for a light by day, the ordinances of the moon and the stars for a light by night, who disturbs the sea, and its waves roar (The Lord of Hosts is His Name): "If those ordinances depart from before Me, says the Lord, then the seed of Israel shall also cease from being a nation before Me forever". Jeremiah 31:35&36.*

113

They have not ceased being a nation in spite of man's constant desire and best efforts to wipe them off the face of the earth!

• *Seventy sevens are determined for your people and for your holy city to finish the transgression, to make an end of sins, to make reconciliation for iniquity, to bring in everlasting righteousness, to seal up vision and prophecy, and to anoint the most holy. Know therefore and understand, that from the going forth of the command to restore and build Jerusalem until Messiah the prince, there shall be seven sevens and sixty two sevens; The street shall be built again, and the wall in troublesome times. And after the sixty-two sevens Messiah shall be cut off, but not for Himself; and the people of the prince who is to come shall destroy the city and the sanctuary. The end of it shall be with a flood, and till the end of the war desolations are determined. Then he shall confirm a covenant with many for one seven. But in the middle of the seven he shall bring an end to sacrifice and on the wing of abominations shall be one who makes desolate, even until the consummation, which is determined, is poured out on the desolate. Daniel 9:24–27.* Sixty nine of these sevens have been fulfilled precisely in history and the last one awaits Gods time!

• *"Fill up then the measure of your father's guilt. Serpents, brood of vipers! How can you escape the condemnation of hell? Therefore, indeed I send you prophets, wise men and scribes: some of them you will kill and crucify, and some of them you will scourge in your synagogues and persecute from city to city, that on you may come all the righteous blood shed on the earth, from the blood of righteous Abel to the blood of Zechariah, son of Berechiah, whom you murdered between the Temple and the altar. Assuredly I say unto you, all of these things will come upon this generation". Matthew 23:32–36.* And they did!

• *And they will fall by the edge of the sword and be led away captive into all nations. And Jerusalem will be trampled by Gentiles until the times of the Gentiles are fulfilled. Luke 21:24.* They did. They were. It was. But no longer is!

114

- *At that time Michael shall stand up, the great prince who stands watch over the sons of your people and there shall be a time of trouble, such as never was since there was a nation, even to that time. And at that time your people shall be delivered, every one who is found written in the book....And one said to the man clothed in linen who was above the waters of the river, "How long shall the fulfillment of these wonders be?" Then I heard the man clothed in linen, who was above the waters of the river, when he held up his right hand and his left hand to heaven and swore by Him who lives forever, that it shall be for a time, times and half a time: and when the power of the holy people has been completely shattered, all these things shall be finished. Although I heard, I did not understand. Then I said, "My lord, what shall be the end of these things? And he said, "Go your way Daniel, for the words are closed up and sealed till the time of the end. "Many shall be purified, made white, and refined, but the wicked shall do wickedly; and none of the wicked shall understand, but the wise will understand. And from the time that the daily sacrifice is taken away, and the abomination is set up, there shall be one thousand two hundred and ninety days. Blessed is he who waits, and comes to the one thousand three hundred and thirty-five days. But you, go your way till the end; for you shall rest, and will arise to your inheritance at the end of the days. Daniel 12:1, 6–13.* It Is Coming!
- *I say then, have they stumbled that they should fall? Certainly not! But through their fall, to provoke them to jealousy, salvation has come to the Gentiles. Now if their fall is riches for the world and their failure riches for the Gentiles, how much more their fullness! For if their being cast away is the reconciling of the world, what will their acceptance be but life from the dead?... Well said. Because of unbelief they were broken off and you stand by faith. Do not be haughty, but fear. For if God did not spare the natural branches, He may not spare you either. Therefore consider the goodness and the severity of God: on those who fell, severity; but toward you, goodness, if you continue in His*

115

goodness. Otherwise you also will be cut off. And they also, if they do not continue in unbelief, will be grafted in, for God is able to graft them in again....For I do not desire, brethren, that you should be ignorant of the mystery, lest you should be wise in your own opinion, that blindness in part has happened to Israel until the fullness of the Gentiles has come in. And so all Israel will be saved as it is written: The deliverer will come out of Zion, and He will turn away ungodliness from Jacob; for this is My covenant with them, when I take away their sins. Concerning the Gospel they are enemies for your sake, but concerning the election they are beloved for the sake of the fathers. For the gifts and the calling of God are irrevocable. Romans 11: 11–12, 15, 20–23, 25–29. You have His word on it!

- *Nation will rise against nation, and kingdom against kingdom. And there will be great earthquakes in various places, and famines and pestilences; and there will be fearful sights and great signs from heaven....Now when these things begin to happen, look up and lift up your heads, because your redemption draws near....so you also, when you see these things happening, know that the kingdom of God is near. Assuredly, I say to you, this generation will by no means pass way till all things take place. Heaven and earth will pass away, but My words will by no means pass away. But take heed to yourselves lest your hearts be weighed down with carousing, drunkenness, and cares of this life, and that day come on you unexpectedly. For it will come as a snare on all those who dwell on the face of the whole earth. Luke 21:10–11, 28, 31–35.* It Is Coming.

In spite of the witness of these *Scriptures* and many more like them, *some of these dearly beloved a millienlists* even yet have no real faith in *God's Sovereignty* over the affairs of the nations of this world. In their heart of hearts they don't believe that:

He is the God of today's events just as he has been the God of all history past.

They, in effect, believe that there is no unfulfilled prophecy that we can understand that is really related to the real events of the end of this age.

To them, His Coming will most certainly be as a thief in the night. It will come upon them unawares. All because we didn't care, didn't pay attention, didn't understand and couldn't warn them in the very simple terms that Jesus so graciously supplied As a naturally following corollary of this, their unstated hypothesis, they also discount all of *His Testimony* (all of *His Prophecies*) about the *historical predicates, sequences and settings* of what He declares to be the *Soon Coming Events of the End of this Age.*

to all of us in *Matthew 24, Mark 13*, and *Luke 21.* Let us hurry to address this failure by presenting the simple facts to them.

A Review of What Was twisted

The facts of the story of the tumultuous times of the end of this age are set forth in clear perspective by Jesus in *Mathew 24, Mark 13* and *Luke 21.* His disciples had asked Jesus in plain terms about the end of this age.

According to Jesus' response, the age ends with a series of astounding events with an unthinkable climax which could never have been imagined or guessed by man, but could have only entered the mind of man through revelation by God. We today wouldn't have a clue of what is about to happen unless He had told them. But He told them, in plain, simple language. To get that message today we only have to *hear Him.*

He gave them the *who, what, when, where, why* and *how.* He gave them the facts with great clarity and specificity. He also let them know that He would provide the believers with an increasing light of clarity, certainty and understanding, as the time of their accomplishments drew near. He indicated that the coming events would become so clear (to the wise) as the end neared, that, as Daniel had said of the very final events of this age,

"The wise will understand." In Daniel's case, for the Tribulation saints, the wise will understand, even to the timing of the very last day. Review the last four verses of *Daniel 12* to bring this truth back to mind.

According to *Luke 21* the faithful will recognize the dawning of the season they have been waiting and longing for and will lift up their heads and look up, ready to receive the redemption which they, and those who are asleep in Jesus, most assuredly will receive before the final crescendo of catastrophes falls on all who yet dwell on the earth.

This is what Jesus clearly presented. But this is also what the adversary has so skillfully twisted that it has become a mystery, a hidden secret, to most today, and indeed, throughout the ages.

Brief Summary of the Misconceptions Wrought by This Deception

By simply overlooking *Luke 21:12*, teachers were, and still are, able to interpret the three accounts of Jesus' Olivet Discourse as being simply three different views of the very same events. In particular, they were, and still are, able to say that all three accounts describe the same destruction of Jerusalem in 70 AD. *Seeing Luke 21:12 destroys this fiction.*

However, from this one erroneous conclusion alone the following confusion (and much associated chaos and havoc) has been wrought on succeeding generations:

- The second coming of Jesus which Matthew says will come immediately after the Tribulation of those days must have taken place in 70AD. This faulty conclusion has resulted in at least three teachings that persist to this day:
    - *He* actually physically returned shortly after the fall of Jerusalem in 70 AD just as He said He would and was either not recognized or was recognized only by the elect and reigns today, recognized only by the elect.

- *He* was only speaking allegorically. *He* came back either as the church, as the pope, as the *Holy Spirit*, or some other way, open to whatever interpretation men might make of it.
- The word *"immediately"* has no trustworthy meaning and we thus have no reliable chronology available to us of these days.
- All prophetic history ended in 70 AD or shortly thereafter.
  - This view supported replacement theology, which held that the church replaced the Jews and that all of the promises that *God* had made to the Jews were bestowed on the church. This doctrine catapulted the Church, as it was then understood and is still understood by millions today, squarely into the middle of the warfare of the kingdoms of men as a competitor for earthly power and rule. Yes, even as the arbitrator of all earthly power and rule! It put the scepter and the sword firmly in its hands.
  - There will be no further intervention by *God* in the affairs of the human race after 70 AD until the indeterminate, unexpected and unheralded instantaneous "end of time". We are on our own in a truly do-it-yourself religion and life. *His Coming* will be like a thief in the night.
  - There certainly will be no signs or advanced warnings of the approach of the end, no special season of anticipation, no reason to watch and pray, as Jesus urged us to do.
- The end time return of the Jews to the promised land and their ultimate salvation is denied in spite of the testimony, among many others, of *Moses, David, Isaiah, Jeremiah, Ezekiel, Daniel, Zechariah, Malachi, Matthew, Mark, Luke, Paul, John* and *God*. Check out *Daniel 12 and Romans 11* for starters. These witnesses are all discounted under the rubric of the church being spiritual Israel.
- The Jews are thus considered disinherited, disenfranchised and dismissed because they crucified Jesus, all in spite of the

eleventh chapter of Romans and the many other testimonies of God just cited.

The Theft of the True Story

Now as strange as it may seem, this plain and simple account of the end of the age from the very lips of our *Lord and Savior* as recorded in these three *Gospel* accounts was lost in the ancient past. To most it is still lost. It is unknown to most who profess to believe in *Jesus*. If it is hidden from them, how dark are the shadows in the realms that lie beyond those who believe, in those regions that depend on their testimony? It has been hidden in plain view by the harmonizers, those who would correct our understanding of the texts and remove all ambiguities, that is, those mysteries (to them) that seemed to be ambiguities (to them).

The plain gospel truth has been muted. It has been disguised. It has been twisted. The plain, unvarnished truth has been rendered a fable. Reality has been reduced to a fairy tale. It has become as Mohammed's midnight flight to heaven, the Hindu sagas, and Grecian mythology. It has been stolen *and yet* still lies hidden in plain view for those who will look. How the perpetrator must laugh as we stumble by the truth in our blindness as destruction approaches. Rather than the truth, it is apparent that we have believed a falsehood, a very traditional, ancient, honored and accepted falsehood.

Grievous Pain and Great Sorrow

The truth of *the plain, clear, prophetic words* of Jesus *has been confirmed* by its steady fulfillment in history. The truth of this matter is, in fact, so plain and so clear in both statement and in fulfillment that, as the *Scriptures* say, a *wayfaring man, though a fool, could not err therein*, but we all have.

Knowing *Jesus'* prophecy and witnessing and tracing its continuous, faithful fulfillment in history, and especially in this age, has been a continuous source of great wonder, great joy and great hope to those who have experienced it. It is especially exciting and comforting *today*, to those who know and *believe*.

However, Jesus' plain prophecy and its plain fulfillment are also the source of grievous pain and great sorrow within the hearts of all believers who seriously weigh this matter today.

Because it is those who claim the Name of Christ who have been the principal instrument for putting out the eyes of mankind and making them blind to these truths and thus to the *Messiahship* and *Lordship of Jesus of Nazareth, Only Begotten Son of God, Alpha and Omega, Prince of Peace, the great I Am, the Word who was and is God.* Of course, wasn't it those who sat in Moses' seat in Jesus' day that blindly led the blind?

How many Jews in the last fifteen hundred years would have believed, if the Christians hadn't hidden the truth? Would there have even been a Muslim religion, if the Christians hadn't hidden it? We have done this by ignorantly or deceitfully hiding these plain facts from each other, from our children and from the Jew, the Muslim, the atheist, the pagan idolater and all others who sometime or other might have had the heart to search out the truth about The Messiah. Offense must come, but woe to them by whom it comes

If not putting out their eyes, we have, at the least, put out the light, snuffed out the only candle, the only lamp, in a very dark place. This shredding of documents, this obstruction of justice, this concealment of crucial evidence has gone on for millennia.

There is no more enduring, self-evident and incontrovertible, proof of the deity of *Jesus* than the continuous fulfillment of *His own prophetic words* in history from the day they were first spoken to this present hour.

What havoc it has wrought. How different history and the events of this present age would be if this truth had not been hidden. But it was. You see, *He spoke plainly of the end. His words were faithfully transmitted to us.* We who have *The Word* and have studied *The Word* then proceeded to scramble *The Word* into nonsense. We managed to obscure it, and thereby we have been accessories to high crime. We have tampered with this evidence from heaven to our own confusion and condemnation, and to the loss of many.

Obviously, we haven't done it all by ourselves. Satan has helped; in fact he has inspired and directed the effort. And our gracious *God*, in honor of *His likeness in us* that *He* put there, has allowed it, but woe be to us who have been the instruments of this matter. We will not be held guiltless; we are responsible beings. *O, God*, in the *Name of Jesus* forgive us.

Dear ones, with contrite hearts and broken spirits do not delay in lighting this light, even now, upon the pathway of all you can before it is too late.

The Shadow, the Blindness and the Veil

Even as Peter pleads with us, *"To hold on to prophecy as to lights in a dark place until the day dawns and the morning star rises in our hearts,"* (the morning star is Jesus, and He rises and His light increases in our heart as our trust in Him grows, as who He is and what He is doing slowly, slowly dawns on us, as we surrender our will, and in its place let His likeness in us rule and direct our hearts), we have not held on. In fact, most of us, most of our lives, if the truth were known, have actually despised prophecy, refused the light and scoffed at those who didn't refuse it. These words of the book judge us, *"For the testimony of Jesus is the Spirit of Prophecy." Revelation 19:10.*

And as the writer of *Hebrews* warns us, *"that a veil lies upon our hearts until we turn to the Lord,"* we apparently have not really turned.

And as Jesus quotes the prophets of old, *"having ears and not hearing and eyes and not seeing, lest they should hear and see and turn and I would heal them,"* we apparently have not seen nor heard nor turned nor have we been healed.

Why have we not?

Because, to a large degree, there has been a *shadow, a blindness, darkness and a veil* upon the teachings and traditions of the church for lo these many years and consequently upon our own hearts and our own understanding as well. We have believed and loved a falsehood. Why? And of more immediate and urgent concern, is it too late to understand and to turn?

Dearly beloved, it soon will be. Remember Jesus' wondering lament in *Luke 18:8*, *"...Nevertheless, when the Son of Man comes, will He really find faith on the earth?"* He is coming soon, very soon. Will He find you eagerly awaiting His appearance or blindly unbelieving and still scoffing?

The hope driving this presentation is that He will find you understanding and believing.

The Limitations of This Presentation

Now God's promises are true and He is faithful. He is also patient. His patience, in fact, is our salvation. Dear reader, He will still graciously lift the veil even in these last days for those who turn to Him with all their hearts, for those for whom Jesus is truly Lord. It is for these that this presentation is intended. It is not intended to be an exercise in persuasion or a debate with the scoffer or the unbeliever. But if you believe in the depth of your heart that God has called you according to His purposes, my prayer is that you let Him open your heart as he opened Lydia's heart on the bank of the river in Phillipi to hear the Words of the Lord, if you find them here.

Remember that wonderful story, how the Holy Spirit led Paul across a continent and a sea, prevented him from going into provinces where the gospel had never been preached, sent him a vision and granted him understanding of it. Then He led him to Lydia on a riverbank. But then, glory be to God, the final critical step was taken, the one without which all of the others would have been totally in vain, *He, the Lord, opened Lydia's heart* to hear the words of Paul. May it be so between the Lord and you.

Agent of the Shadow,
the Blindness and the Veil

But first, some questions that cry out for an answer. Why were we blinded? How did it happen? Who blinded us? Who has told and so effectively perpetuated the falsehood that we so love? Who would be the agent of the deceiver to deceive? Who would the deceiver choose to bring the shadow, the veil, the darkness to enslave the children of *God*, by and to, this great falsehood? And how would he entice his agent to act so darkly?

What would be the reward he would offer for such an act of treason against all of mankind? Who would he enable to initiate a scam that would have sufficient legs to carry it to the end of time, not only subjecting the world thereby to murder and mayhem in every generation along the way, but to carry it all the way to the end and thus to especially condemn the vast majority of the final generation (more than half of the people who have ever lived, I am told) to a sudden destruction such as has not been experienced since the days of *Noah*?

Why was the lie originally told and then propagated by retelling all these many centuries?

The plain overall purpose has been simply to destroy man, all of us, to steal our inheritance and to destroy us. But, for this plan to succeed it has been necessary to hide it from us. The lie has thus been obscured over the centuries as it has been passed through the minds and hearts of succeeding generations. This obfuscation has been played out on many different fronts in many different guises to layer on the confusion or maybe, even especially, the somnolence and to make it stick. We have been put to sleep.

Our *Creator* endowed us with remarkable powers and, indeed, even a true likeness to *Himself.* Therefore the attack on man to seduce Him away from *God*, generation after generation, must be multifaceted, yet coordinated, relentlessly sustained, and indeed vicious and executed without conscience to succeed.

And it has been.

However, most of those actively involved in the conspiracy have probably not really understood what they were doing. Our prayer is that The Master who extended grace from the cross, in His final appeal in the flesh to the Father for mercy for sinful mankind by pleading, *"Father, forgive them, they do not know what they are doing."* may extend it even yet to all of us.

The Creation of a Myth

One strategy of the lie that seems especially targeted on the last generation was to create an aura of mythology about the events of the end. This is just what the science (falsely so-called) of evolution has accomplished in making *God's Record* of the beginning as if it were also a myth. Thus the liar, in the same way, has made a parable, a fanciful tale, rather than a reliable history, out of *God's Record* of the end.

Mythology at the beginning and mythology at the end! Most Christians are rendered thereby no better off than the Hindu and his fairy tales. Most modern Hindus know that their stories are not historical. They are just fanciful tales belonging to the unscientific past and to children. Because of them, however, the Hindu turns his eyes to his idols and has been blinded to seeking the true living *God*, whom even the Christians have helped obscure from his sight.

Christians have joined them with mythology at the beginning and mythology at the end, with man left to consult with Himself and his equally unreliable co-dependents to determine how he should go in the middle (between the ends) where he lives out his little lost play of life with little purpose and precious little trustworthy direction.

If *Jesus* is not to be trusted with the past and the future, He is not *God,* and *His* teachings are just platitudes to be weighed and judged and applied as we see fit. *He* just joins the pantheon and *His* religion is just one among many, and we have the same hope as the idol worshipper. This is exactly the view that the Hindu has of the Christian. I wonder where the Hindu got it? This prevalent ambivalent view among Christians concerning their God also wonderfully reinforces the view of Muslims that we are, in fact, essentially polytheistic idolaters.

> You can believe what *He* said about the beginning and the end, simply because everything else *He* said about world history has come to pass *in order and on time*. Check it out!

Jesus proclaimed the true historicity of *Genesis* when *He* confirmed, *"at the beginning, He made them male and female"*. *Jesus* also declared the true historicity of the events of the end, when on the Mount of Olives He said, *"But before all these things..."*

As if making a myth out of the *Word of God* and thus cutting man loose from any certain moorings and leaving Him aimlessly adrift in pitch darkness, vulnerable to every attack were not enough, the removal from his conscious knowledge and memory of the true story has, if possible, an even darker side.

It has literally been the mediate cause and means of enslaving much of mankind to thoughts, philosophies, values and, ultimately, systems of religio-government with resulting acts of history that are antithetical to *the Christ* and *His Kingdom*. These are the acts of the enemies of *Christ*, bent on snuffing out *the Spirit of God* on earth and with that act, bringing about the damnation of *His children*.

Disclaimer

A disclaimer is needed here because we are about to enter into a realm that depends on a recovery of memory of events from the distant past and I am not really sure how all of these things really played out. I am not a historian. As is usual with mankind, I am guilty of many of the things I have charged others with. For example, many of the things that you will read here I have simply heard or read from others, who, although closer to the scene of action by almost a score of centuries, still were not eyewitnesses

126

and who undoubtedly entertained some bias in reporting the things they thought they knew. In fact most, if not all, of the ancient "authorities" were compromised. I'm not talking about the Scriptures here, but the writings of men.

Thank God for the *uncompromised* Word of God

Some translations of copies of the originals of these "authorities" were consulted. Even so, I still lack the background to fully interpret the meanings, not knowing the circumstances and forces operating in those long gone days and who the players were and what their real agendas were. I have certainly over-simplified the flood of events, the torrent of human activities and even the scant records of them that are available to us. I haven't even read nearly all of the pertinent documents that are available to me, even in English, my only language.

If we had another decade or so, perhaps I could mend some of these flaws. I believe, however, that although I may miss some significant turns, the trace of the overall story is not greatly distorted. And we don't have another decade.

However, don't hang your hat or your faith on what you read here. *Hang it on the* sure *Word Of God. God had His Son, The Eternal Word,* say, *"But before all these things...."* that you can trust!

An Example of What Was at Work in the Past and How it Came Down to Us?

For example, it is commonly accepted by those who have read, that Augustine was a leading light of the western church in setting forth doctrine and in leading the spiritual life. He is not only recognized as a father of the Roman Catholic Church, perhaps its leading doctrinaire, but was also relied on by both Luther and Calvin to support these pillars of the Reformation, and thus he is recognized as a spiritual father of the Protestants as well.

It was Augustine, so I read, that took *Jesus'* parable found in *Luke 14:16–24* of the man who gave a great supper and invited many who offered excuses and didn't come, then sent his servants to the highways and hedges to seek the poor, maimed, lame and blind *to compel* them to come in so his house might be full and used it to build a doctrine of compulsory conversion.

If this is true, this teaching must have been a guiding light to all the princes of the church and kings of the realm who, we are told, did these very things for centuries thereafter, (and probably before) forcefully converting men to *their own* concept of a christ against their will and even little children against their knowledge. Even Mohammed who came on the scene a couple of centuries after Augustine was also apparently his disciple, at least on the issue of forced conversion. Apparently so was Calvin on this very point as well. At least it is said that he agreed to the death of Servetus who taught doctrine contrary to his own. Was this why he was called the Pope of Geneva?

It is ironic that as Augustine was laying on his deathbed in Hippo, this African Christian city of his bishopric was under siege *by Christians.* These besieging Christians were of a different doctrinal persuasion from Augustine. They were Arians. Augustine was not. They had been brought by ship from Europe by a prince who imported them to fight his battles. He must have been an Arian because they immediately began to lay siege and eventually conquered the strongholds of the non-Arian faith along that coast.

These Christian Arian warriors were of the tribes called Vandals. History likes to remember them as vandals, not valiant Christian warriors, contending for their faith. Interesting, isn't it? They opposed the popular western doctrine of the Trinity which had been formulated fairly recently by those whom Augustine called fathers. They got their vandal reputation, not from their orderly dismantling of Roman treasure in the great city, which they did, but from the ferocity of their attack against Trinitarian property in Africa. It was against the other sect that they fomented, not against the common culture!

Although these Arians had a disagreement with Augustine's party on some matters, they were apparently in total agreement with Him in his doctrine on using the sword to win the argument and settle the issue. Talk about the chickens coming home to roost in dear old Hippo!

Augustine's *compulsion* doctrine, drawn from a parable of the *Prince of Peace,* may not have originated the use of the sword in church matters, but it certainly legitimized it. The church was already encouraged to use the sword in the defense of the state. James explains how these things rose so quickly among believers and persist even to this day,

Do you not know that friendship with the world is enmity with God? Whoever therefore wants to be a friend with the world makes Himself an enemy of God.

"Where do wars and fights come from among you? Do they not come from your desires for pleasure that war in your members? You lust and do not have. You murder and covet and cannot obtain. You fight and war. Yet you do not have because you do not ask. You ask and do not receive, because you ask amiss that you may spend it on your pleasures. Adulterers and adulteresses! Or do you think that the Scripture says in vain, "the Spirit who dwells in us yearns jealously?" James 4:1–4.

Don't neglect these verses or make the mistake of dismissing them as allegory.

History has proven them otherwise!

Conversion of the Kingdom

Now lets plunge head long into the distant past and see what was there. Satan, the prince of this present world, is in mortal combat with the Prince of Peace whose kingdom is not of this world. Jesus had told Pilate, *"My kingdom is not of this world. If My kingdom were of this world, My servants would fight, so that I should not be delivered to the Jews: but now My kingdom is not from here."* He had also told *His* apostle, *"Put up your sword in its place, for all who take the sword will perish by the sword. Or do you think that I cannot now pray to My Father and He will provide Me with more than twelve legions of angels?"*

Now in those days Satan was really having his way on this earth. The earth was full of pride, hate, fear, greed and lust, just as it is today. It was full of war whose roots were in just these things. *Jesus* had resisted these very temptations from Satan in the wilderness. He defeated Satan then, and He defeated Him again in the tomb, rising and then ascending.

After rising He breathed His Spirit on His own faithful few, and then in heaven at the throne of God He received from the Father the power to give the Spirit to all of His own on earth, so He sent *the Spirit* down from *heaven* into the *hearts of His own* to indwell them, to save them, to preserve them, and to empower them to carry on the fight.

Now the battle raged in the time of *Daniel's* fourth beast, *"dreadful and terrible and exceedingly strong, with great iron teeth, devouring, breaking in pieces and trampling the residue with its feet."* The *kingdom of heaven* against the kingdom of the prince of this present age.

Constantine, who soon reigned over the fourth beast kingdom, may not have originated the idea of making the kingdom of God a military auxiliary to the kingdom of men, but he certainly coveted the physical and potential martial power of the saints that dwelt in his kingdom. And all of the old religions had always been the vassals of the throne, the handmaidens of the kings, had they not? How could he enlist this power in the martial service of the empire when for years they had refused to even defend themselves by martial means against the empire? *How could he rip them away from their allegiance and devotion to the Prince of Peace to join him in his wars?*

These people, whom the beast had ravished until the passing of Diocletian, had suffered passively, as the world sees it. But they had not been passive or cowardly. They had just fought the battle on a different plane with different weapons, following in the footsteps of their *Master* who had instructed them to turn the other cheek. He had taught them to love their enemies, to do good to them who despitefully used them, not to resist evil, but to overcome evil with good.

He had said His kingdom was not of this world. He was called by His own, Lord, and by the ancient prophets, *the Prince Of Peace.* He had told them that the Kingdom of God would not come with signs to be observed, neither would they say here it is or there it is *because He said that the Kingdom of God is within you.* It would be an *internal spiritual kingdom made of righteousness, peace and joy in the Holy Spirit. It would literally be God's dwelling place on earth, and it would be in the human heart.* They bowed down before Him and kissed Him and crowned Him King of their lives.

How could the state co-opt *heaven's kingdom's Ruler* that dwelt on an entirely different plane to fight the battles of earthly power and glory (read lust, pride, covetousness, envy and greed)? Since Satan could not do it in desert or tomb, obviously they could not do it either.

But they could effectively isolate His followers from Him and lead them into their camp by quenching *the Spirit* in their hearts and dulling *its Sword* in their minds. *His Word, the Scriptures,* would have to be dulled and twisted because on the surface it would appear that the formula, the doctrine, the means of this transfer of *the kingdom of heaven's* power for the use of this earth's kingdoms military ambitions is not to be found in *them.*

Look carefully at *The Beatitudes,* the rest of the *Sermon on the Mount,* and *the rest of all that He had to say.* Look especially at His very life, how He lived. It is just not there. God is not flesh and blood. *God is Spirit* and *He seeks those who would worship Him in Spirit and in Truth.*

According to Jesus and the prophets:

His kingdom is invisible. It comes without observation. It is within you. It is in your heart. *Luke 17:20,21*

His kingdom is spiritual. The length, breadth and height of its dominion lands are: *righteousness, peace and joy in the Holy Spirit.* These *three spiritual dimensions* are the dimensions by which the Kingdom of God is defined and its extent measured. *Romans 14:17.*

The warfare on behalf of this *spiritual kingdom*, to defend its borders and to enlarge it, to which He calls His *saints* is also spiritual. Their weapons are to be: *truth, righteousness, the gospel of peace, faith, salvation, the Word of God, and prayer. Ephesians 6:13–18*

To equip the saints to wage this war, God through His Son broke the seal of sin that separates man from heaven and sent the Holy Spirit down into the hearts of those He adopted so that they could bear the fruit of His Spirit out of the good soil of renewed human hearts, which *fruit is love (which brings with it) joy, peace, long suffering, kindness, goodness, faithfulness, gentleness, and self-control. Galatians 3:4–7; 5:22,23.*

This fruit of God's Spirit, which is also Spirit, is Love. Love implanted by the God who is Love in the human heart is the True Spiritual Reproduction of God Who is also Spirit. God, Who is Spirit and Who is Love, begets Himself in the human heart that has been cleansed for this very purpose by the blood of the Lamb to be the Holy Temple of His dwelling… You must be born again. The Father and the Son dwell in us through The Holy Spirit They have given us. They truly dwell in those born of the water and the Spirit.

On the other hand, in sharp contrast, the Scriptures plainly record that God had ordered the *sons of Israel* into physical flesh and blood battle to conquer the physical land that He had promised them. He promised them victory and gave it to them time after time in history.

Too bad that it wasn't Judaism that was growing by leaps and bounds in the Roman Empire. Now, if the state could tap that authority and power that seemed to belong to Israel under the old covenant and somehow transfer it to the Christians under the new covenant! But how?

Truly it appeared that there was a great disconnect between the *Old Covenant* and *the New*. *God* truly had a new thing in mind for the followers of *His Son. Something like the world had never known.*

The Methodology of Conversion

If only the Scriptures could be shown to endow *this bold and brawny new faith* with all that *power of earthly dominion* that *God had promised and delivered to Israel*! What a powerhouse that would create! So a great exercise in scriptural legerdemain was called forth to steal Israel's inheritance and to give it to the church. Make the church spiritual Israel, perhaps seizing upon passages such as *Galatians 6:16*. Declare fleshly Israel foreclosed on, disinherited and dead, seizing upon certain passages in the letter to the *Hebrews and other Scriptures*.

Then steal and transfer to the church all of the promises of earthly power given in *the Scriptures* to Israel. Having appropriated Heaven's prerogatives, declare that *Jesus' kingdom* is now of this world and call His servants to fight. Then freely and boldly go raise your armies and taxes and set up and set down earthly kings and take physical dominion over the earth in the name of Christ. Create the fiction of "Christian" kings and kingdoms (and republics) and equate them to the *kingdom of heaven*. Then convert men to Him by the sword or the rack or any other convenient device at the king's disposal.

Declare that the destruction of the Temple, the cessation of the daily sacrifices, the destruction of the Jewish nation and the scattering of the remnant to certain death in the arenas and permanent banishment in 70 AD and 135 AD *to be the forever, God-ordained, end of the Jews*.

But make sure that *Luke 21:12* and *Romans 9, 10* and *11* are out of sight.

Then promote the miraculous ascension of the church to supreme worldly power under Constantine in AD 332 as *God's* seal of anointing to make this transfer complete.

Did not God give Constantine a sign in the sky shaped like the Greek letter, Chi (X) which, being the first letter of Christ in the Greek, the emperor took to stand for the Christ? (ref. W. E. Vine's Expository Dictionary), and did not the heavenly voice say that he was to conquer by this sign? Did not this sign and voice from heaven seal God's approval of the church as an earthly kingdom, authorized to wield not only the imperial scepter but the sword as well? At least that is the story told and the efficient effect of it down through all these gory centuries.

In light of the fact that *Jesus, the Prince of Peace*, had said that *if His kingdom was of this world, then would His servants fight*, all the while declaring the good news of the *kingdom of heaven* which according to *Romans 14:17* consists of *righteousness, peace and joy in the Holy Spirit*, is it possible that this fabled story could have been based on the voice of the deceiver, not God? Note that the *Chi* was soon replaced by the catholic cross, which was not a symbol of the Christ at all, but of his crucifixion. This symbol which was soon emblazoned on the shields of the latter day warriors of the cross, including the infamous Catholic crusaders, more closely approximated the Greek letter *Tau* (T)

It did not derive from the simple stavros or stake upon which Jesus was stavrosed (not crucified) but rather the more Ancient *Tau*, sign of the resurrected God Tamuz, son of his virgin mother, queen of heaven, and fertility goddess, Ashtar, after whom the celebration of the resurrection of verdant life in the spring is named, if you would believe it.

All of this devil's brew straight out of the ancient rebellion of Nimrod, founder of Nineveh and Babylon, the original post-flood anti-christ and the originator of both humanistic world government and demonic world religion whose tentacles practices, beliefs, signs and even words reach even to us in our own day, and that, with renewed vigor. Is this connection clear?

Whether it was actually a lying apparition in heaven or the concoction of a later generation to support a *fait acompli* really made little difference to those who lay dying in their own gore in the dust in the hatred and death harvested on and by both its supporters and its victims and their avengers throughout all these long ages.

When the *"if"* of the *"if my kingdom were of this world, my servants would fight"* was removed, the conversion was complete. Ask the victims of the conquerors of the last 1700 years if the sword has truly advanced God's kingdom of righteousness, peace and joy. Ask the victims. They are legion: the Jews, the Orthodox Christians, the Mohammedans, the Protestant Christians and those (even the Catholics) they in turn persecuted, following as obedient daughters in the steps of the mother church. Ask the victims of a hundred Inquisitions and a thousand massacres. Ask the attackers, the counter attackers, the perpetrators and the avengers.

Did the sword advance God's kingdom of righteousness, peace and joy in the Holy Spirit, the kingdom that comes without observation and that lies within the human heart?

Removing the Scriptures

But the Christians believed the *Word of God*. How do you separate them from this, *the Sword of the Spirit*, their surest weapon, their mighty stronghold, their fortress, the transfer agent of their faith, their link to the heart and mind of *God*?

Some of the means employed in working this problem of separating man from The *Word of God* from ancient times are easily recognized and have been amply reported throughout the ages. Physically destroy the people's *Bibles*. Destroy the people's confidence in their own understanding and in their own common sense. Make sure that they don't learn to read. Chain the *Bible* to the pulpit. Prevent the *Bible* from being translated into the language of the people, and when that fails, be sure to monopolize the translation of the *Bible*, allowing *authorized versions* only to be circulated and read.

Distract the people with games and opportunities and worries. Co-opt them with power and wealth. Bring into the church by the sword and other inducements many unregenerate aliens. Dilute, isolate and if necessary even kill those who still seek truth and understanding.

135

History records that all of these evils have been done. Satan and his minions are desperate that people not know what is in the Book. Why? In the resulting vacuum of *spirit* and *knowledge* promote the idea of specialists in holiness and in understanding. Borrow an old trick from the pagans and also pervert the Jewish order again. Create and elevate a priesthood. Create this elite to think, to interpret, and to decide the *Will* and the *Word of God* for the common man, to stand in the place of *God* in the hearts and minds of men.

Let this order of priests, in fact, be holy men for them, to take their place before God, so that the common man may then be free from the demands of holiness to pursue worldly matters, including those of interest to the state, especially those interests of the state which are in conflict with the *Rule of God* in the *hearts of His sons.*

And, oh yes, don't forget to remind the common man that he is common, just a clod, not, dearly beloved, the *Inspired Creation of God in His Own Image.* Lead him to believe that God doesn't really want to commune directly with Him as *His own very precious child*, as *Jesus said*, but instead, has provided a gaggle of intercessors, dead and alive, who do have His ear and for a price will have a word or two with Him for us commoners.

Having effectively separated man from his God by *destroying the effectiveness of God's Word in his life*, then, like a blind man, lead this poor captive by the hand to his destruction. Never let Him understand that the *Word of God* says that *he, the believer Himself*, is a *Royal Priest* that stands daily *offering the living sacrifice of his own body and of the praise of his confession* before *The Living God*, the *Only Father* that he has, *Who* alone forgives his sins and makes him Holy, and that Jesus, *his very own brother* is the *only mediator* he truly has or will ever need.

This brief recounting identifies at least some of the elements of the very effective master plan of the accuser of the brethren and goes a long way in explaining the blindness and darkness of heart and will and mind and sight that so broadly encompasses so very much of the world to this very day and is not missing from a very large swath of the nominal Christian community.

Who has he not enlisted in this seduction from before Constantine to this day? Which king, nation, tribe, hierarchy, sect, church or apostasy has clean hands? Which have not done the bidding of the prince of this present world, the prince of the power of the air, the spirit that now works in the sons of disobedience? Satan has had almost universal assistance from us all. After all, he is the prince of this present age.

And it has been a very effective campaign. He has very effectively separated man from his God by removing the Word of God from his mind and from his heart.

The Age of Ignorance

How else can you explain the near total ignorance of many vital elements of *God's Word* among *God's* people in this, *the information age*? How many have read, pondered, thought and prayed to understand why *Romans 9, 10* and *11* exist where they exist and say what they say. And what in the world do we think is the *antecedent* of the *"Therefore"* that begins the much beloved 12th chapter of Romans, wholeheartedly embraced by the Gentile Christians? What indeed is the antecedent?

How else can you explain the almost total universal blindness to the notoriously invisible *"But before all these things."* of *Luke 21:12*?

Why would the adversary care about these particular chapters and verses anyway? Why would he care whether we saw them or not? Why?

Because *if these verses were left to stand* in the broad light of day and truth, the inescapable conclusion is that God is not through with the Jews yet. The promises (and the curses) still stand. The church is not Jacob, is not fleshly Israel and never has been. And God is not through with human history. He will still undoubtedly require an accounting by the usurpers of stolen identities and properties.

Suddenly the ancient, easily manipulated, quaint old *God of the Bible* unexpectedly and uninvitedly lands squarely in the middle of today's bloody and astounding events. *He* is no longer held cooperatively docile and impotent behind the corral fence the other side of 70 AD where He can do no more harm than a fairy tale. And where *He* certainly doesn't have to be reckoned with in any serious manner on a day to day basis. How rude and inconvenient of *Him* to uninvite *Himself* to stay home in ancient history where He belongs.

If these verses stand.

From the adversary's point of view, it is essential that these Scriptures be invisible, along with many others. But these, in particular, if seen by those who have eyes to see would unravel his scam of replacement theology and all its devastatingly invasive tentacles almost instantly. So he has paid very special attention to hide them. And he has done a fantastic job of it.

Because *God* is not through with the Jews yet, He is not through with the world yet, and that means us. How terribly inconvenient. God is out of His box. And we haven't got a clue of what to do with an uncontrollable and rampant God, *a God who insists on being God*. We just may be forced to fall on our face (before it is too late) just like the ignorant, benighted third world pagans do when faced with a natural calamity they cannot understand.

So What?

So what if Jesus did make the end time sequence a very plain history simply told before the fact, rather than intentionally making it a mysterious babble subject to any fanciful interpretation that any cult or generation might want to place upon it? What are the consequences? Does it really matter? What difference does it really make in how I live out my life? What difference does it make? I'm living the best way I know how, and I don't have the energy to sort out the correct answer on this matter anyway, so tell me that it just doesn't make any difference.

138

Besides all that, good men and scholars have been on both sides of these issues, haven't they? And besides all that, we have, these many years, believed the good men on our side. Do we have to open the discussion again? Didn't our very good forefathers settle it for us many years ago? Can't they be trusted?

Do We Have Grounds for Questioning?

Before we address these questions of relevancy themselves, we must address the very grounds upon which these questions can be asked in the first place. We find ourselves in asking them standing very much in the place of *Job*. Simply because we cannot fathom the *Mind of God* nor have been taken into *His Counsel* are we to presume that He frees us to disregard *Him* or *His Instructions* for us? Are we free to obey only that which falls into the realm of our own understanding or with which our reason agrees? If this is the case, what does Faith mean? When and where do we exercise it? What place does it have? Is it banished? Does reason take its place?

Is our knowledge, experience and understanding so perfected, exercised, matured and completed that we might begin to think of ourselves as being equal with *God*? Might we even challenge *God* to a contest, confident of the outcome, Are we saved by faith or not? Or does our very own reasoning, independent of *God*, save us? because we have a more balanced view, a longer perspective on history now, more facts now, better data, newer and more modern means of analysis leading to better understanding? Are we, in fact, superior to *Him*, with a better plan, maybe, even a superior (more tolerant) righteousness?

Or are we in our self-imposed blindness simply following our traditions, which are, *themselves*, grounded and advanced, one generation after another, in nothing more substantial or profound than *themselves*. Even worse, once launched on the basis of human reasoning, they take on a life of their own, evolving generation after generation. Having no higher authority, they are subject to continuous amendment and embellishment by their godmen keepers, who are just like the myth maker/playwrights of ancient Greece who reinvented their gods on a seasonal basis in ever more exciting script to keep the crowds coming back to the theater for more.

In addition to considering these hideous, blasphemous thoughts that, in fact, lie just below the surface, only slightly camouflaged, we also need to ponder if *God* would waste *His* and our time, precious *Scriptural* shelf space and the power of the *Holy Spirit*, not to mention our own very limited devotion and power of concentration, to tell us things that don't make any difference? Would *He* weigh down our relationship with *Him* and our very lives, with the clutter of useless *Scriptures* that have no meaning or that really don't make any difference?

We need to ponder these questions seriously as we review our attitudes toward *God* and *His Word* in these, or in any other *Scriptures*.

Dear Christians, Did He say, "Whatsoever a man sows that he also shall reap?" Did He say, "That he who sows to the flesh shall reap corruption, but he that sows to the Spirit shall reap everlasting life?"
Yes, He did.

Relevancy

Now, finally, to the question of relevancy. Is an understanding of *Jesus' Declaration* that gives title to this *Part III, "But before all these things..."* really worth the effort it takes to unravel the musty bonds that have obscured it for so long and held it invisible to so much of the race? Is the statement that it makes really worth the effort to hear and understand? Does understanding it make any real difference in how I understand the past, the present and the future and especially how I live out my life? Does it affect my faith, my view of *God*? Or, more importantly, *God's* view of me? Are my values and my view of myself affected? Are my relationships with time, with people, and with *God* really impacted? If the answer to any of these questions is "yes", then we should proceed with determination and haste.

Please go forward with me; give me the opportunity to show you why I believe, in fact, that many of these issues are directly and emphatically impacted by this message, which has been so effectively hidden from our eyes by the crafty adversary these many years. The fact that he has tried so hard to hide it says volumes about its importance. Let us see how we can best organize this relevancy inquiry.

First, the Details

First let it be noted that the following conclusions are derived directly from the sequence of the end of the age events proclaimed by Jesus and brought sharply to our attention by the declaration in *Luke 21:12* "*But before all these things they shall lay their hands on you, and persecute you, delivering you up to the synagogues, and into prison, being brought before kings and rulers for my name's sake.*" and the apparently very sharply contrasting account in *Matthew 24:9*, where we read "*Then shall they delivery you up to be afflicted, and shall kill you: and you shall be hated of all nations for my name's sake.*"

The operative event-sequencing words, paired in these two verses, i.e. "*Before*" and "*Then*", set the timing of the events to which they refer, relative to the signs of the commencement of the end of the age Tribulation, just as surely as if they had been "before" and "after".

Consequently the *Scriptures* can only be understood to reveal that the whole series of events related by *Luke* must come before the signs which herald the end of the age can even begin to appear. Whereas, in great contrast the events related by *Matthew* must follow after these signs of the beginning of the onset of the Tribulation, and thus they are part of the End of the Age Tribulation.

If this timing, as clearly presented by Jesus, is clearly understood, then many other things will be clearly understood and fall into place as well, including the fact that the rapture of the true believers will occur, without further warning, at the very beginning of the creeping onset of the Tribulation's leading indicators. *That means it is imminent right now.* As Jesus promises in *Luke 21:28, "Now when these things* (i.e., the signs they had asked for and that He had given them in *Matthew 24:7* and *Luke 21:10* and *11) begin to come to pass, then look up, and lift up your heads; for your redemption draws near."*

Remember, *Luke's* account, which also facilitated the believer's escape from Jerusalem in 70 AD *(21:20),* states that the very dawning of the *Last Day Tribulation Signs* is the *Lord's* notification that escape from this still future holocaust is imminent. However, we are instructed this second time not to flee to the mountains of Judea but simply to look up and lift up our heads because we don't have to flee, He is coming for us. The mountains of Judea will not be the refuge of the true believers this time, but heaven itself.

In huge, stark and ominous contrast, in *Matthew's* Olivet account there is not one word of warning or promise of escape, not a word, not a sign concerning the destruction of Jerusalem *either* in 70 AD or of the coming holocaust. *Matthew's* only message is to the Jewish (and Gentile) remnant that fails to take the early route out. This message comes deep in the throes of the middle of the end of days Tribulation, not to seek escape from it but to persevere in it. They are to flee Jerusalem to be preserved in a hiding place of *God on earth.* They are to be faithful to the end, when, as promised *(Zechariah 14, Revelation 19, Matthew 24, etc.), Christ* will descend on the Mount of Olives and fight as in the day of battle against the antichrist and his minions, bringing the Tribulation to its close.

Luke alone, which was primarily written to, and read by the Gentile Christians gave the necessary prerequisites and details of the first two escapes (70AD and the coming Rapture), but did not even mention the third escape from the middle of the Tribulation. He didn't need to because his primary audience will be witnessing these final struggles from Heaven.

In contrast, very few of *Matthew's* primary audience of slow of heart and dull of hearing Jews have yet to read this very special treatise designed especially for them by their ever faithful *Father*, even to this late date. And not many more of them will read it before the Tribulation begins.

However, once the Tribulation has started, many will pour over it, and by the time of the Great Tribulation that is heralded by the sign of the Abomination of Desolation, spoken of by *Daniel, the prophet and Jesus, the Messiah*, standing in the Holy Place, it will be their most prized possession, strength, guide, and the vessel of their hope. They will flee to the mountains of Judea to await their Savior, faithful to the end.

In the meantime *Matthew*, Gospeller to the Jews, wastes no space whatsoever in issuing what would be futile warnings of the impending destructions of 70AD and the coming Tribulation (and the wondrous and rapturous routes of escape available to those who hear and *believe*) to those who can not hear and will not read and will not believe.

Imminency

If the story truly told by *Jesus* is truly understood, then the doctrine of imminency, i.e., that *Jesus* could return at any time, with no historical precursors whatsoever, which was taught for many centuries, although thoroughly refuted in the Scriptures especially by *Paul* in the second chapter of *II Thessalonians* is finally shown to be false. The stealth verse of *Luke 21:12* clearly reveals that this doctrine was not applicable at all until June 1967.

Luke 21:24 is the last verse of the series of verses which, starting in *verse 12*, contains the events which Jesus said must be finished before the signs of the end can begin. This last verse contains the closing event of this series. And what does this final verse of the precursor events say? It says, *"And they shall fall by the edge of the sword, and shall be lead away captive into all nations: and Jerusalem shall be trodden down of the Gentiles until the time of the Gentiles be fulfilled."*

No one questions that *the first half of this verse as well as the four preceding verses* describe the destruction of Jerusalem by the Romans under Titus in 70 AD. Now *the second half of this final verse* of the series covers the history of Jerusalem from its destruction in 70 AD to some distant time that coincides with the *fulfillment of the times of The Gentiles*. At that time, the trodding under foot of the city will cease. We do not know exactly what *"the time of The Gentiles be fulfilled"* means or precisely when it occurs. There are at least three possibilities that might be considered.

The first is, that the time of The Gentiles is simply that time which is allotted to The Gentiles to trample Jerusalem down and that it expires when they no longer trample Jerusalem.

However, if the designation, "Gentiles" is taken as it was first used in *Scriptures* in the table of nations of *Genesis 10*, it may mean the end of the worldwide dominance of the descendents of *Japheth* or the Europeans in world affairs. From Alexander to this generation, *Japheth's* descendents have been the undisputed rulers of the world. Since the *Genesis 9* blessings and curses of *Noah* also include Japheth's descendents dwelling in the tents of *Shem*, it may especially refer to the fall from dominance of the Europeans over the Middle East.

World historians note the collapse of the European worldwide empires since WW II, and we all know of the erosion of Western dominance over the desert oil barons since 1973. Has the time of The Gentiles as predominant in world affairs been fulfilled, or are its closing days being fulfilled as we watch?

Or does the times of The Gentiles being fulfilled have to do with the mystery of *Romans 11:25* where the fullness of The Gentiles coming into the kingdom of God, is given as the precursor of all Israel being saved?

Or is it all three?

As subject to question as to what the meaning and the timing is of *"until the times of The Gentiles is fulfilled"* (and it is a timing question), there is little debate among historians as to when the trampling of Jerusalem under foot by The Gentiles ceased.

This linked event to *this question of timing* in this verse occurred on June 7,1967.

Since June 1967 we live in the *post-verse 24* era. Dearly beloved, there are no prophesied events left that lie between today and the trumpet call of *God* to those that belong to *Him*, whether in the grave or alive, except the very faint beginnings of the birth pains of the final Tribulation. As Jesus urged, *watch and pray.*

The Eminent Effect of the
Misplaced Doctrine of Imminency

This doctrine of undifferentiated imminency down the ages aided and abetted the dealers and promoters of the *myths-of-the-end* by *obscuring* any references to *true history* by *Jesus*. Did not the endless and baseless announcements of His Coming devalue the truth of *His Coming* in the minds of those so deluded and all the others who witnessed or heard about these announcements and their related frenetic activities? Do not these earlier false and disappointed hopes seriously cloud the minds of those who might otherwise take Jesus' words about the present age at face value?

Truly understood, the story in *Luke* clearly reveals that we are the first generation that can, with Biblical support, truly anticipate that we are the final generation. Therefore, the *watch and pray admonitions of Jesus* apply directly to us as to no other generation that has lived since these words were spoken.

We are brothers to the people of the generation of *Noah* and brothers to the generation of *Jesus* who lived or perished in the Days of Vengeance in Jerusalem in August 70 AD. We should live in the hope of *Noah* and of the earliest *Christians*, who by faith in their hope escaped. But we, with an exceedingly greater joy and expectation because our escape is not just to another polluted place, but to the pure light and absolute joy of everlasting life in the presence of Jesus and God Himself, and that *now, finally, imminently.*

Some Other Considerations

So what? Some might still say? You have simply related some historical highlights. What exactly is there of any really practical consequence to your argument? Some might still say that they cannot detect any practical effect, one way or the other, of either accepting by faith *Jesus' Words* on this matter or rejecting them. We are all Christians, they say. We are doing the best we can to live the Christian life. One is not condemned or saved by accepting or rejecting some controversial argument, so why waste our time. Just get on with life.

This kind of argument really appeals to us. But remember that by his deception, lo, these many years we have been conned as a people into believing that the issue is complex and subject to many different interpretations, including the strong possibility that the whole thing is a myth. And the doubters and scoffers point to the array of interpretations of prophecy among the 'true believers' to certify their skepticism. Satan's 1700 year-old campaign is bearing fruit just in time in this final and fateful age for which it was especially designed. The damage done by Satan is not just to harden the doubter, but also to confuse the believer.

You see, in obscuring the plainest of facts as set forth by *Jesus* in *Luke 21:12*, our enemy has removed the certainty of truth from the believer's own personal arsenal against Satan. He has armed the scoffer against *the believer and his Lord* and has removed the sturdiest weapon of Scripture that the believer possesses today to prove the *Divinity of Jesus*.

When the brethren scoff at each other, the doubter has a free pass. Let me say plainly, brother scoffer, your disdaining of the *plain Word Of God* (and it is plain and those of you who have looked at it know that it is plain) simply because you personally cannot see its practical usefulness is a witness to the success of Satan's campaign in general and against you in particular.

Look, we don't know for sure how far the fearful signs that precede the Tribulation will be advanced before *God* takes the expectant believers of *His* up and out of here. Incidentally, weren't all the virgins waiting on the bridegroom believers? Some were ready. Some were not. Some got to go that night, the others, at the very best, maybe got a second chance. On the Day that is coming there will be weeping and gnashing of teeth, especially among those who will know that at the very best they may be getting a second chance, but for certain missed the first.

We don't know how far into that time that will eventually surpass all other times of human experience in magnitude of fear and devastation that the expectant believers must go before redemption. But it will be advanced enough for those who are real believers, who are really expectant, the true watchers and prayers, to know, without doubt, these worst of all times are, in fact, beginning.

The case has been made that the excruciating details of the Tribulation given in *Matthew 24* are recorded in advance in order to strengthen and comfort those who must endure the Tribulation, faithful to the end in order to be saved. Might not the beginning of the early warning signs that Matthew calls the birth pains serve the same purpose for the early believers, especially if the rapture doesn't come until deep into these birth pains?

Perhaps the early signs are given so that those who await the rapture will not grow fearful and lose their confidence in the Lord at the very last moment, but they will have the courage to stand still and see the salvation of the Lord, just as the Hebrew children were admonished by Moses at the parting of the Red Sea as Pharaohs's army came thundering down upon them.

The standing still part of the rapture may be the greatest test of faith a man will ever face. It will certainly defy all human reason and even sanity. It will attract ridicule and scorn, laughter, derision and in some cases, maybe even murder. It will be an act that has no other basis or support but the solitary individual's utter abandonment to his God. It will be viewed by the world as worse even than suicide bombing. Stephen's sacrifice will be replayed. We need to discipline our hearts in every matter of life today to say, with *David* and our *Master*, *"Father, into your hand I commit my Spirit."*

Perhaps those who say that an understanding or an acknowledgement of the significance of *Luke 21:12* is not necessary for their well being will have an opportunity to reconsider these thoughts as these fearful beginnings come crashing down. They will then suddenly realize that *Luke 21:12* was brought to their attention to give them a basis of hope as they see all their earthly supports and expectations dashed, and these dreadful things approaching.

But even then it will still be *a matter of the heart. God* did not give *His only begotten Son* so that those who have the technology, or worldly wisdom, or a secret formula or special knowledge could figure out salvation. No, *He* gave *His son so that whosoever believes in Him should not perish but have everlasting life.* Knowing the time and place of *Jesus'* birth did not give Herod a leg up on salvation. It did not save Him. Don't be caught playing around with this.

"Know this first of all that in the last days mockers will come with their mocking, following after their own lusts, and saying, "Where is the promise of His coming? For ever since the fathers fell asleep, all continues just as it was from the beginning ..."
II Peter 3:3,4.

To say that the recognition and the study of the chronology of *Matthew 24* and *Luke 21* is not important may be equivalent to saying that since we haven't noticed anything different yet, we certainly are not going around looking for signs of trouble, when *He said, "watch and pray."*

How do you read the record? Is *God* someday, without warning, going to zap the whole world and catch as many as *He* can unprepared? Or is *He* still in the business of seeking and saving that which is lost, desiring that no man be lost, but that all be brought to repentance? Is *He*, as *He* always has done, going to plead, warn and give notice to those who are alive at the time of the coming judgment? Did Noah build the Ark of salvation and warn the people for 100 years of the coming destruction? What about *God*, Jonah and Nineveh? Did not Abraham plead for a recount in Sodom and Gomorrah, and then weren't angels sent to retrieve the righteous before the destruction?

Will God zap or warn?

How do you come down on this question in light of *His character, record*, and especially *His promises* in the *Scriptures about these days?*

Why did He say watch and pray?

If the Great Tribulation is beyond human experience as *Jesus* tells us that it will be, and its coming will be recognized by the expectant watchers, we could expect that even its faintest beginnings will somehow have upon them the mark of unprecedented calamities, so that they can **How can you say you believe *in Him* if you don't believe *Him*?** be distinguished from all earlier national and ethnic conflicts and all other natural calamities of famines, earthquakes and pestilences and thus truly be seen and understood to be signs of the end.

On the other hand since the time frame of the arrival has been so carefully identified by the Lord, perhaps the beginning of the signs of the beginning of the Tribulation don't have to be so extraordinary for them to serve *God's* purpose for His faithful watchers. Are such signs now observable? Many believe they are. Are they now extraordinary compared to other ages? Some say, yes, they already are.

Even non-believers, non-Christians predict unprecedented epidemics, wide spread famines from unprecedented worldwide climate changes and uncontrollable population growth. The humanist Club of Rome has long predicted that our population explosion is on a collision course with the earth's resource base, which will be unable to sustain life for the teeming billions in just a few years, certainly within the lives of this generation. And nothing can be done about it.

Earthquake activities have never before seen the attention they now get on almost a daily basis. Not a week passes without news of devastation in one or more corners of the globe. The records show that the occurrence of major earthquakes, those of 6.5

magnitude or greater on the Richter Scale are, in fact, on a world wide basis increasing exponentially. See the earthquake watch feature in the Drudge Report on the Internet for the latest, literally up to the minute, account of these activities, worldwide.

Incidentally, two thousand years ago only *God* knew that those longing for His coming could depend on knowledge of "earthquakes in various places" as a useful sign of the *beginning of the end* and a warning that *the rapture* was at hand. Instant knowledge of "earthquakes in various places" has not been available to any generation in all of the history of the world until *this generation.*

The same is true of the knowledge of national and ethnic conflicts, epidemics and famines. Read your daily paper, watch your nightly television news or better yet tap the internet, *www.wnd.com* or the *Drudge Report*, and read almost every English language newspaper, wire service and commentator published that day on the globe. Yet, others doubt.

On the other hand consider this, with *Jesus* telling us that we can begin expecting these signs only after June 1967 do these signs have to be extraordinary to alert the watchers? Maybe. Maybe not. But, probably they will. Maybe they already are. Pay attention. *Watch and pray.*

When *Jesus* tells us to expect something that we have never experienced, the last thing we should rely on is our experience. We may find ourselves like the three descending from the mount of transfiguration that wondered among themselves, fearful of asking *Jesus* outright what *He* meant by *"His resurrection."* They did not understand. They had no experience on which to rely. As for the Tribulation, our understanding cannot rely on our experience either. It must rely on His Word. When all else fails, just take *Him* at *His Word*, even if you don't understand it. We can't go wrong doing that.

Let Us Try One Last Time, Stealth Verse Luke 21:12

Dear reader, *Luke 21:12*, the invisible verse, is the simplest and clearest of all Scriptural proofs that the destruction of Jerusalem and the Jewish nation in 70 AD were not the end of the Jewish nation. Neither were they the final and complete fulfillment of all of the prophecies concerning the Jewish people and nation. (*Romans, chapters 9, 10* and *11* undeniably confirm this. If they do not confirm this, what do they mean? More about this later)

This verse as it sets the scene, is a part of the simplest and clearest of all *Scriptural proofs* that the world as a whole and the Jewish people in particular yet face a time of unprecedented testing and destruction before *Jesus'* descent to earth on the last great day of this age, the day of judgment and salvation.

This verse clears up and demystifies the jumbled tangle of end time events that have plagued human understanding for these many centuries, an understanding that was jumbled up simply because *this one verse* has not been seen, read nor believed.

This verse is the plain language of Jesus, without figure of speech or symbolic content. *It requires no interpretation. It only requires belief.* Jesus just tells it as it is and as it is going to be. Believe it or Jesus will come as a thief in the night for you at an hour that you know not, and you will be caught unawares just as He has warned us. We are saved by faith.

A sincere believer's reading of the chapters, *Matthew 24* and *Luke 21*, in light of the sequence of events declared in *this one verse* properly sets the stage for understanding the terrible time of the end. It also will reveal that the rapture of the true believers will occur early on, at or near the very beginning of the onset of these terrifying things.

In brief, the first phrase of this verse, *"But before all these things..."* sets the events that *Luke* then enumerates in *verses 12 through 24*, including the destruction of Jerusalem in 70 AD, chronologically *before* the signs that according to both *Matthew*

151

and *Luke* come before the final cataclysmic period which also, according to *Matthew*, includes the next (another) desolation of Jerusalem, the one which is yet to come.

Once the impact of this order of events is understood and appreciated, *these two chapters* unveil a wealth of end time information that *God* intends for us to have *now*, including the setting of the rapture in the sequence of the end time events.

The stealth verse, *Luke 21:12*, has been called the invisible or sleeping verse because so many scholars have read right past it, totally ignoring it, in their search for meaning and coherency in the *Mount of Olives Discourse*. Pages and pages of commentary have been written on these chapters, but seldom a single word about *verse 12* and its stage setting, *"But before all these things..."* Lengthy attempts to try to equate *Matthew's 24:15* *"the abomination of desolation standing in the Holy Place"* to *Luke's 21:20* *"armies encircling the City"* occupy these commentaries, but often not a single syllable addresses *Jesus'* clear proclamation through *Matthew 24:9* and *Luke 21:12* that these strikingly dissimilar events were not only not the same, but they wouldn't even occur within 1900 years of each other.

How far off can you get. One of these is an event marking the middle of the end-time Tribulation, which hasn't even begun yet, and the other is an event which indisputably occurred as Titus' encircling armies crushed the city 1932 years ago.

How About Whole Stealth Chapters? How About Three of Them in a Row?

But *Luke 21:12* is not the only verse sacrificed on the altar of destroying the historicity of Jesus' plain teaching. How about whole chapters of one of Protestant Christianity's favorite books? How about the stealth chapters of *Romans 9, 10* and *11*?

What are the stealth words that lie after the *fantastic promises of chapter 8* upon which our *hope of salvation* depends and which culminates in these words, *"No, in all these things we are more than conquerors through Him who loved us. For I am convinced that neither death nor life, neither angels nor demons, neither the present nor the future, nor any powers, neither height nor depth, nor anything else in all creation, will be able to separate us from the love of God that is in Christ Jesus our Lord."*

What lies after this culminating shout of Christian victory? And upon what is based the famous *"Therefore"* that introduces the shouting declaration of the Christian life charter of the beloved 12th chapter of Romans.

Christians all strive with all their might to conform to the total sacrifice of these marching orders, *"Therefore, I urge you, brothers, in view of God's mercy, to offer your bodies as living sacrifices, holy and pleasing to God. This is your spiritual act of worship. Do not conform any longer to the pattern of this world, but be transformed by the renewing of your mind. Then you will be able to test and approve what God's will is, His good, pleasing and perfect will."*

What is this *"view of God's mercy"* that supports the *"Therefore"* that commences this awesome call to Christian living, which reaches the moral crescendo of: *"Do not be overcome by evil, but overcome evil with good."*

What lies between *chapter 8* and *chapter 12*? No less than the stealth chapters of *Romans 9, 10* and *11*. Read them now, many for the first time, and weep for yourself. Many self-confessed *Bible* believing Christians have not read these chapters. Many self-proclaimed *Bible* teaching churches have not taught these chapters.

What is the Connection?

Then again ask yourself why. Why have we not seen nor noted these chapters except for a proof text every now and then? Maybe you will find a hint when you examine the very close connection between the stealth verse of *Luke 21:12* and the stealth chapters of *Romans 9, 10* and *11*.

The connection is, they both deal with the promises of God to the Jews.

And, of great significance, they deal specifically, with those promises to the Jewish people, which have not been fulfilled yet, which means that *God* is still active. *He* isn't finished with the Jews yet, and *He* is not through with directing human history.

There is still a reckoning for the nations and people, a reckoning that *He* has carefully laid out before us, as *He* always does. *"God doesn't do anything without telling His prophets before hand."* Amos 3:7. This means that God's Scriptures are still full of things He wants us to know that still lie ahead. *If He tells us, He wants us to know.*

What kind of response to *the Almighty God* is it to say, "Why do *You* want to burden me with this knowledge?" I was doing quite well in my ignorance, thank *You*. Keep these dreary (and scary) end time things to *Yourself*. I had rather *You* just surprise me some day, you know it is appointed to man once to die and after that the judgment. Just make it quick and as painless as possible. Isn't that what you are saying?

Isn't that response just like the one made by those, who in the days of Noah, might have said, *"Noah, we have had enough of your weather forecasts. Just let us alone. If it rains, it rains. We will look to our own canoes if it comes to that, thank you very much."*

Or is there an even more sinister plot to destroy among Christians recognition of *God's* dealings with the Jews in this day. Or maybe an even more sinister one yet: to have the Christians, themselves, once more try to destroy the Jews.

Dear reader, has Satan ever used the Christians to try to destroy the Jews? Yes, dreadfully, many times over. What Satan couldn't do in the garden, Pharaoh in Egypt, Hamman in Persia, Antiochus IV Epiphanies in Jerusalem, Herod in Bethlehem, Satan in the wilderness and in the tomb was assigned to the semi-Christians in Rome, Madrid, London, Paris, Moscow, Warsaw, Berlin and thousands of lesser known places and pogroms. Is he through using Christians to destroy the Jew? Apparently not. *Watch and weep and pray.*

Light to the People in Our Own Day: A Jew and a Mohammedan

Those of you who do have a passion for the salvation of the Jewish people, you have been greatly handicapped, even in your zeal, if you have not seen and believed the *Stealth Scriptures.* One bright young Hebrew man told me recently that he confessed *Jesus* as *Messiah* not very many years ago when he was shown that *Jesus* indeed looked to the end of time and clearly foretold the history of the Jews from the Mount of Olives to the present day (and beyond).

The young Hebrew in the innocence of faith saw clearly. He easily recognized that only *God* could see the end from the beginning and reasoned and confessed that *Jesus* must be *God.* When the true historicity of *Jesus'* teachings about the future are restored through seeing and believing *Luke 21:12*, then the road is clear for the Jew to see their national history played out just as Jesus said it would be, so far. The proof of the *prophet* is in the fulfillment of *his prophecies.* The proof of the *Messiah* is that *He* could tell *the end from the beginning.*

But that is not all. Leave *the Scriptures* alone and let them speak for themselves and any man can see plainly, if he will.

God once greatly blessed our lives by bringing an eighteen year old Mohammedan boy to live with us. He stayed for almost two years. We could speak very little Arabic, he, very little English. When Betty challenged Him to learn about Jesus, his only resource was a *Bible* in Arabic.

He read *The New Testament* by Himself in two or three days without eating or apparently sleeping. As soon as he finished reading it, he came bursting into the house saying that he loved that *Yesu* and asking for another book about *Him.* We told Him that the *Bible* was the only book that told the whole true story. He was amazed at this and responded by rushing out again and reading the *New Testament* all over again in two days. He did not eat. Again he may not have even slept. When he finished this second time, he came bursting into the house again, saying, "I *want* this *Yesu.*"

I thank *God* to this day that we had no other books and that we didn't speak Arabic. This devout young Mohammedan, skilled in the Koran, came straight to *Jesus* without human intervention. He didn't have to wade through two thousand tormented years of obscuring twisted human doctrine. He missed the blessings of the harmonizers. I guess that he just thought it was all true.

By jumbling up the accounts in *Matthew, Mark* and *Luke* to "harmonize" them, such devastation has been done. We have totally obscured what *Jesus* intended to be so plain that a wayfaring man though a fool would not err in it.

When the harmonizers were through with *Jesus' Words*, nobody could follow *His Discourse*. It lost its historicity, became mythology, a fairy tale, an allegory of the great battle between good and evil and an ageless pep talk to keep the faith, good will overcome and some day the church will be victorious. It became very Hindu, very new age. It became very generalized, very non-offensive, very lowest common denominator, very acceptable.

It put *God* out to pasture and restored man to his cherished place in the center of everything. Christianity and its book became very human and very humanitarian. *That is not what it is. Nor what it says.* But we have made it so and that is the way we like it. We will call *You* when we need *You, God*. In the meantime disappear behind *Your* screen because we don't want to see *You*. What children we are. What mischievous children.

Why would unaided men who could read and write and who were acquainted with *The Scriptures* and who set themselves up to guide mankind into all knowledge of *God* do such things? Why would they poke out the eyes of generations with a stick?

The truth is that they were not unaided. The father of lies is the source of all lies, and since this whole mess is a lie from beginning to end, it is evident that these men were not unaided at all but moved as they were inspired to destroy the Jewish Nation, to destroy the Christian hope. Will they be successful? They have been. What course lies ahead? What will be the answer to *Jesus'* question, *"Nevertheless when the Son of Man comes will He really find faith on the earth?"* Work for the night is coming.

What is the Substance of Faith?

You ask, what difference does it make whether we understand and teach *These Scriptures* or not. Does it make any real difference to the well being of the church and to our own efforts to live a Christian life? Even if the present state of your communion with *God* does not give you a clear answer to these questions in your own mind yet, in the meantime, before you reach a hasty decision, ponder why you would even consider letting Satan get away with a lie that has taken the truth away from the children to whom *God* sent it at such great expense?

On the other side of the battle, Satan has spent great energy in devising this lie and propagating it. Hadn't we better be on *God's* side and oppose Satan even if we haven't yet figured out what all the issues they dispute are really all about? Isn't this what faith is all about? Kind of like what Abram's journey from Ur of Chaldees was all about. We love that story of faith.

The Question of Relevancy, again, in History

If you think that these *stealth verses* and *chapters* have no significance, then can you say that you have any concern about the tragedies that have been caused by hiding them? Hiding them, both historically and in this present age? Historically you can trace the disenfranchisement and attempted extermination of the Jew to the ideology created by those whose interest was best served by destroying *These Scriptures.* You can trace the rise and continued preeminence to this day of the state's age-long and world-wide manipulation of the *Holy People of the New*

Covenant to do its bidding by the conversion of the stake to the sign of the cross, to the sword and the scepter.

And this, to the people whose Leader said, *"My kingdom is not of this world. If it were, then would My servants fight."* You can trace this vast, ancient and almost unchallenged movement to this same crowd, to this same stratagem. *And again this stealth verse and these stealth chapters must be neutralized to make it happen.*

The Question of Relevancy, again, in the Present Age

Even in this present age, the *Preterists*, the predominant school of interpretation in most of the churches of today, insist that any prophesy that had any historical truth in it was fulfilled for both Jew and Gentile alike in 70AD. And that there is no word of prophecy left unfulfilled today. There is no not one, yet to be fulfilled by *God's Acts* on this earth or in heaven, except the one that says that it is appointed unto man once to die and after that the judgment.

This most popular position cannot stand if the *stealth verse and chapters* come to light. They must be hidden from the people. It is an imperative. And they are!

Now most a millenialist and post millienialists today do not identify themselves as Preterists, leaving that classification to a new style of interpretation that boldly claims that teaching and gladly accepts all of its drastic consequences. These are consequences that the Old School has avoided by fictionalizing the hard parts.

However, both Old School and Neo-Preterists have in common the belief that most, if not all, of Matthew 24 was fulfilled in 70AD. This is the common belief that is the cornerstone of the Preterists' structure of interpretation, whether old or new.

Does It Make Any Difference?

Let us assume that you are a leader in a church of this *Preterist* tradition. If you are a Christian leader, most likely you are, since most churches follow this teaching. What will it cost you to see, read, understand and *believe*? Don't think that it will only cost you an hour or two of fervent study and prayer.

It may very well cost you the companionship of your dearest friends. It may cost you your family, your church, your place of honor, your position, your leadership, your priesthood, your pastorate, your eldership, your name, your reputation, your respect, your life.

Only the truth is worth that price. But with truth comes freedom and salvation. It is a bargain, and you will never find yourself asking, "What difference does it make that these Scriptures are brought to light, even, or maybe, especially, at this late date?"

The Preterists

Present day *Preterists* are the spiritual descendents of the state churches of the fourth century. Their belief system is one of the oldest non-scriptural relics surviving to this day. But survive it has indeed. In fact, today, worldwide, it dominates the thoughts, values and views of the vast majority of those who profess to be Christians.

The Preterists' position underlies the mainline sects and is found in many others. It is foundational to the theology of post millenialism, a millenialism and replacement theology.

There are many nuances to these various creeds, many branches, many sects. Many individual adherents may not even fit the pattern of belief ascribed to them here. It gets quite complicated, but if any part of a faith system is based on the Preterists' supposition, to that extent it is fatally flawed.

A simple understanding of the end-days chronology as clearly presented by Jesus in *Matthew 24* and *Luke 21* utterly destroys the Preterists' basis of all such persuasions. the common error is the belief that *God* essentially fulfilled all of the outstanding prophecies of the *Bible* in 70 AD or shortly thereafter. They reach this conclusion by equating the destruction of Jerusalem by Titus in 70 AD as prerecorded in *Luke 21* with the devastation of Jerusalem foretold in *Matthew 24*, which, according to Matthew's record, is yet to come and does not come until immediately before the *Return of Jesus*.

They can only make this equation if they *totally ignore Luke 21:12* and gloss over many of the other apparent discrepancies of these chapters that appear if the two records are assumed to report the very same events.

All of these positions basically require that their adherents convert the world to the Christ of their understanding, Christianize the world and spread Christian civilization, government and enlightenment to the far corners of the globe, in order to prepare the world so that their Christ might return. They say that when we have got Christian government on earth and a just society in all the world ready, then the king will return either to reign on earth, or more likely just to call us all home to everlasting life in heaven with a "well done, good and faithful servants." They are the children of Constantine and Augustine.

The consequence of this colossal error is the belief that *God* has already done all that *He* said *He* was going to do on earth in the way of intervention in the affairs of this world until the end of time. Therefore, it is up to mankind or Christianity to bring about the kingdom of God on earth. God is gone and won't be back until judgment day.

In extreme cases, until recently, time was seen to essentially have no end and God no plan, but to pick up the dead as they fall off the end of the never-ending conveyor belt at the end of their lives and place them in their eternal abode. According to these, God certainly does not intervene, does not direct the affairs of nations or the feet of men. As a corollary, man and man's governments are in control here. Is there any wonder that man and his governments love this doctrine and hide *Luke 21:12*?

These are all old positions, embraced by Christian kings and governments in very ancient times, one worlders, Christian humanist and just plain humanists and do gooders of all ages, and lately, by the advocates of the new world order. You probably recognize that some of these movements have more non-Christians in them than Christians.

As a matter of fact the world has pretty well co-opted the Preterists' thesis and have just gone the next logical step of denying the existence of God at all. If they must do it all themselves anyway and God has not been operative since 70 AD in fulfilling any of His promises, why not simply throw away the symbolic God, the old idol of the Preterists and their pretenses?

The secularists reason that the whole religious apparatus is just a bunch of non-productive overhead expense anyway. Why not just cut it out and get on with the reconstruction process ourselves? Thus Preterism has been the fertile soil out of which even Communism has sprung. Isn't Communism, which is a mutant of the God-denying, self-relying branch of latter day secular Judaism (Carl Marx first studied to be a Rabbi), based on the same practical conclusion of do-it-yourself, God isn't interested and won't be back for a long time, if ever?

For many, especially in Europe during and after World War I, the blind Christian Preterists' conclusion that under the benevolent ministrations of institutional Christianity that every thing is getting better in every way every day came crashing down under the weight of crushing reality.

Rather than abandon the false doctrine underlying this false hope and returning to *Jesus'* plainly declared order of history, Christians in Europe basically abandoned their faith in God, period. They threw the baby out with the baptismal water. That is how strong a grip the false Augustinian post-millenial (and its Protestant/secular first cousin, a-millenial) doctrine had on the people so long indoctrinated.

They had been taught so long and so persistently that *Jesus* didn't have anything meaningful to say about real history, which, even then, they were so crushingly experiencing, that they could not see. They had been blinded by the long application of the lie. So they just abandoned the whole of *God's Word* as error and fantasy and turned to the other post war Gods of dissipation, drugs, alcohol, Hedonism, Nihilism and Communism that so flourished in the roaring 20's.

The roaring 20's in turn became the hopeless 30's leading to the horrors of the 40's, then to the mutually assured destruction of the Cold War and its many fatal sideshows around the world for the next forty years, and on and on in rapid rampant moral degradation and every kind of personal and national instability to this present day.

So much for the kingdom of God on this earth and man's ability to bring it about by his own effort.

America, of fair isolation to the grossest of Satan's plagues, even to this late date aided by short memory and a surfeit of wealth (which always blinds) and distractions and entertainments (read: bread and circuses) is, to a large degree, still blind to its fate.

Don't think for a moment that the sinister disappearance of *Luke 21:12* from our collective consciousness is simply an innocent oversight or maybe just a mistake, or worse, just of no interest nor moment at all. The kidnapping of *this verse* (among many others) is, instead, a deadly ploy (among many others) of the great enemy of all mankind. Don't be an aide and abettor and a perpetrator of this multi-millenial crime.

The answer to the world's problems all of these years has not been a more efficient program, be it church or state, peace or war, to administer justice and equity and to establish peace, But a heart that loves *Jesus* more than life and trusts Him for everything. This is very personal, and *the human being who has such a heart is the only institution on the face of the earth that is qualified to be called Christian.* This human being is the Holy Temple of God on this earth. In Him the Father and the Son dwell through their Holy Spirit whom they have given Him. Their reign in his heart is the only expression of the Kingdom of God on the earth in the present age.

If Jesus' descriptions of the last days are taken at face value, all of man's still projected improvements in the general welfare of mankind at large are false. Yes, technological progress can be expected and enticing benefits dangled before us, but be sure that the net end effect will be enslavement and devastation until we are rescued by *God's only begotten Son, Jesus of Nazareth.*

The Spirit of God and Prophecy

The connection

The ancient and perpetual strife between and among those who *discount prophecy* is not a curious thing, but it is to be expected, because the interest of those who discount prophecy is focused on the affairs of this world, even though this interest may sometimes be cloaked in religious garb.

"For those who live according to the flesh set their minds on the things of the flesh, but those who live according to the Spirit, the things of the Spirit. For to be carnally minded is death, but to be spiritually minded is life and peace. Because the carnal mind is enmity against God; for it is not subject to the law of God nor indeed can be. So then those that are in the flesh cannot please God. But you are not in the flesh but in the spirit, if indeed the Spirit of God dwells in you. Now if anyone does not have the Spirit of Christ, he is not His." Romans 8:5–9. "But the natural man does not receive the things of the Spirit of God for they are foolishness to Him; nor can he know them for they are spiritually discerned." I Corinthians 2:14.

The truth of these Scriptures is often demonstrated by those who do not earnestly ask God for the *Holy Spirit*. You see, they almost always also discount *prophecy*. Is there a connection between a diminished influence of the *Spirit of God* in mind, heart and life and the discounting of *prophecy*?

On the other hand, let's set the question in a positive way. Is there a link between the Indwelling of the Spirit as promised by Jesus in *Luke 11:5–13* to those who earnestly and continuously petition God *and* a love of prophecy, which is a longing for the Master's return and any word, any sign, of His Coming?

These are curious questions. It is curious that we should even feel compelled to have to pose such questions in the first place in light of the connection between the Spirit of God and prophecy, which is repeatedly set forth in the Scriptures.

There is a profound connection *In The Scriptures* between God's gift of the Holy Spirit and *God's* gift of Prophecy, and thus there is also a profound connection between the gift of His dwelling in our hearts through His spirit and the gift of a love and a desire for His prophetic word in that very same heart.

The connection between God's gift of the Holy Spirit and God's gift of prophecy is clearly set forth in *Revelation 19:10* and *John 14:16,17 & 26* and many other places.

"And I will pray the Father, and He will **"The Testimony of** *give you another Helper, that He may abide* **Jesus is the Spirit** *with you forever, the Spirit of Truth whom the* **of Prophecy"** *world cannot receive, because it neither sees* **Rev. 19:10** *Him nor knows Him; but you know Him, for He dwells with you and will be in you." "But the Helper, the Holy Spirit, whom the Father will send in My Name, He will teach you all things, and bring to your remembrance all thing that I said to you." "No prophecy of Scripture is of any private interpretation for prophecy never came by the will of man, but holy men of God spoke as they were moved by the Holy Spirit."*

In fact all Holy Writ is of the Holy Spirit since it is written, *"The Word of God is the Sword of the Spirit. A divider of soul and spirit, a discerner of the thoughts and intents of the heart."*

The arm of flesh does not wield the Sword of the Spirit, for it is written, *"though we walk in the flesh we do not war according to the flesh. For the weapons of our warfare are not carnal but mighty in God for the pulling down of strongholds."*

And as it is written: *"Eye has not seen, nor ear heard, nor have entered into the heart of man the things which God has prepared for those who love Him. But God has revealed them to us through His Spirit. For the Spirit searches all things, yes, the deep things of God."*

It is not curious that those who have not the Spirit of God heed not the prophets for we know that those who have not the Spirit have not Christ for it is written, *"Now if anyone does not have the Spirit of Christ, he is not His."* Therefore dear brothers *"Examine yourselves as to whether you are in the faith. Test yourselves. Do you not know yourselves, that Jesus Christ is in you?—unless indeed you have failed the test."* II Corinthians 13:5.

The Father and the Son dwell in us through their Holy Spirit whom They have given us, for it is written; *"We are His witness to these things and so also is the Holy Spirit whom God has given to those who obey Him." "The love of God has been poured out in our hearts through the Holy Spirit who was given to us."*

"God is Spirit." John 4:24
"God is Love." I John 4:8 and 16

He has poured out His Spirit, His Love, His Own Self, His Very Own Life into the vessel of our heart. If we reject the *Spirit of Prophecy*, we reject the *Testimony of Jesus*.

Please understand from the *Scriptures* that *the Spirit of God* and *Prophecy* go hand in hand, for literally, One is the Sword of the other. *The Spirit is the Author of Prophecy.*

"For those who live according to the flesh set their minds on the things of the flesh, but those who live according to the Spirit, the things of the Spirit. For to be carnally minded is death, but to be spiritually minded is life and peace. Because the carnal mind is enmity against God; for it is not subject to the law of God nor indeed can be. So then those that are in the flesh cannot please God. But you are not in the flesh but in the Spirit, if indeed the Spirit of God dwells in you. Now if anyone does not have the Spirit of Christ, he is not His." "But the natural man does not receive the things of the Spirit of God for they are foolishness to Him; nor can he know them for they are spiritually discerned."

Indeed the Spirit is the author of the whole Word of God, which is the whole of prophecy. You can't understand *The Word* without *The Spirit.*

Unless God's Spirit dwells in you, the Word of God is foolishness to you and you cannot understand it. So seek the Lord, your God, with all your heart and with all your might, with all your soul and fervently ask Him to give you His Spirit.

Let's examine these deeper issues in the context of *a whole other world.*

A Whole Other World

For a moment let us leave our struggle with the dim, distorted, sordid conception of the world as perceived in the imagination of man and thus unfortunately reflected in the resulting sad history of the world and the chaos that reigns in this present day.

Let us, for a moment, breathe some fresh air of God–created reality.

There is an almost universal law which reigns in the entire physical universe which is recognized by engineers and scientists. It is called the Second Law of Thermodynamics. It is thought by some to be, indeed, universal.

There are many ways to illustrate and to express the Second Law. For example, it is credited with preventing the development of the perpetual motion machine. You see, no device can produce more work than the energy that is put into it. All machines are less than 100% efficient. Heat-producing friction robs the machine of being perfect. You put in a certain amount of energy in terms of fuel or electricity and you get out so much work, say in the miles an automobile travels. But guess what, you get out only about 35% or less of the energy you put in, in terms of useful work, if it is a man-made machine. All the rest goes up in friction-generated heat or out the tail pipe as disorganized waste and heat.

For the same reason, water runs down hill, only. Energy may change forms, but in the end-state of all physical transactions, things are hotter (heat is a very low quality form of energy).

They are not only hotter, but they are more disorganized. We know it as wear and tear. Things do wear out. That is the Second Law at work again.

Another way to look at this manifestation of the Second Law is to note that things tend to disorder, whether it is a house that refuses to sweep itself or a bed that just stays unmade unless some planning and energy is invested (at diminishing returns - no 100% efficiency here either) or whether it is an explosion in a factory. You see, explosions only blow things apart. They can not assemble things. Things have to be assembled by planning and (inefficient) effort.

Now the Second Law applies to the whole physical universe, not just the devices and activities of man. It applies even to the distant stars. Everything, every physical transaction is less than 100% efficient, which means that in every transaction of man and nature, heat, the lowest form of energy is produced and accumulates. Efficiency is less than 100%. Wear and tear takes place. And disorder is increased. Sounds like the end of the world as we know it, doesn't it? The Global Warmists have got it all wrong. They don't think on a grand enough scale. It is not global warming. It is *universal warming*. All of physical matter is warming.

Now, however, there are two exceptions in the whole of the physical universe to this otherwise Universal Second Law of Thermodynamics. These exceptions are strangely connected only to this one small planet on which we live. More specifically, they are strangely connected to *life* on this one small planet on which we live. Uniquely, to life and to life only. Strange, indeed.

You see, life and life alone has the extraordinary ability to take the scattered randomness of the resources that surround it and to gather it and reorganize it into the most complex of all known structures, chemical transactions, electrical systems, command and control centers and systems, symbiotic relationships and operations. It reverses the explosion, creates splendid order out of lifeless disorder. Life is the First Exception to the Second Law of Thermodynamics.

And in man, and man alone, the Second Exception to the Second Law of Thermodynamics is uniquely and wonderfully expressed. Man, in the likeness of his Creator, was gifted by Him with the extraordinary ability to think abstract thoughts. To think, to plan and to execute.

There are only two phenomena in the universe that buck the trend ordained by the Second Law of increasing disorder and increasing heat that seem destined to eventually roll up this old worn out universe like a scroll to be tossed away. These two exceptions are life, which regenerates itself, and higher abstract thought, which links prior knowledge, observations, conclusions, planning, direction and execution to bring out of randomness, works of art and utility.

The *Creator* is not subject to the creation or to the laws thereof. *He* must have grand fathered *Himself* out! And then He bequeathed to man, by special creation, *His Own Supra Nature, Life and Mind.* And, if we let *Him, He* will also give us, by special adoption, *His Spirit* and opt us totally out too, to a realm beyond the writ of the Second Law where there is no wear and tear, nor sorrow, death nor tears.

That is the truth that lies behind *Jesus'* extraordinary exhortation that you must be born again - outside this realm of the Second Law. You must ask *Him* to give you *His Spirit*, which comes from beyond the writ of the Second Law from another place that is no place at all as we understand it, and He will.

Ironically, speaking of two specific sites in a land that is most disputed today, for which men slay each other to preserve the right of worship there, Jesus said, "a time is coming in which you *will worship God neither on this mountain nor in Jerusalem... Yet a time is coming and has now come when the true worshippers will worship the Father in Spirit and Truth for they are the kind of worshippers the Father seeks. God is Spirit, and His worshippers must worship Him in Spirit and Truth."*

The only true and acceptable worship of God is Spiritual; which is a loving, devoted, connection; a oneness with Him; Spirit to Spirit; Spirit from, by, through, of and in Spirit; a continuous true heart-sharing with Him, One on One, in a realm known only to Him and to those who through rebirth have entered that "other place" with Him. Worship takes place neither on the mountain nor in Jerusalem or any other appointed place here below.

This intimate sharing is being One with Him even as the Son is One with Him; One heart, One mind, One life by and through His One Holy Spirit whom He has given to us through His Son and to all who obey Him and through Whom we live and in whom we move and have our very being, and by whom we will also be raised from the dead, should we sleep before He comes.

His kingdom is not of this world. It does not come with observation. It is neither here nor there. It is within you. It is in your heart. Its composition, its dimensions, its contents and its boundaries are righteousness, peace and joy in the Holy Spirit, all given to you by God. It is not of this world; if it were, His servants would fight. We are indeed in this world, but not of this world, and our warfare and weapons are not carnal, but mighty in God for pulling down strongholds...and...bringing every thought captive to the obedience of Christ. Those who hear Him and so answer His call and so relate to the King are the general assembly and church of the First Born, the sheep of His pasture, the betrothed to His Son. This is His Edah and Qahal, this is his Ekklesia and Paneguris that He came to build and the gates of hell have not and will not prevail against it. It is sealed in heaven and its members are registered there.

"He who did not spare his Own Son, but delivered Him up for us all, how shall He not with Him also freely give us all things. Who shall bring a charge against God's elect? Who shall separate us from the Love of Christ? Shall Tribulation, or distress, or persecution, or famine, or nakedness, or peril, or sword: as it is written: "for Your sake we are killed all day long; we are accounted as sheep for the slaughter."

"Yet in all these things we are more than conquerors through Him who loved us. For I am persuaded that neither death, nor life, nor angels nor principalities nor powers, nor things present nor things to come, nor height nor depth, nor any other created thing, shall be able to separate us from the Love of God which is in Christ Jesus our Lord."

The prospects of increasing technological dominion and widespread peace and prosperity on this earth and in this life are nothing but illusions of satan to attempt to enslave the world. What it will really accomplish is the diversion the world's attention from what is really happening so that the Day of His Redemption will come as a thief in the night and catch them unawares and they will be trapped on earth to be victims of Satan's final outrage and God's ultimate response.

Those who are saved on the earth in those days after God has called His own home will truly be refined by fire. If Satan can't ultimately win, he will at least create as much devastation as possible. He is the ultimate suicide bomber.

True liberation comes only by Jesus. Our job is not to conquer the world for Christ by the sword or any other means, but simply to love God with all our heart, mind, body, soul and spirit and to love our neighbor as our self; to confess His Name before men and angels, to attest to, and obey the truth of His teaching, pray for deliverance from temptation and hang on until He comes, letting Him dwell through His Love in our life in sharing with the needy, loving mercy, doing justly and walking humbly before Him, loving our enemy, caring for the sick, the widows and orphans, keeping ourself unspotted from the world, defending the defenseless, overcoming evil with good, and most of all accepting His forgiveness for our sins as we forgive those who sin against us. And all of this not by our power or strength, but indeed by a surrender of these very things to His sovereignty and power. for it must indeed be God who works in us both to will and to do for His good pleasure or it is all man made and in vain.

The General Assembly and Church of the First Born

(The paneguris and ekklesia of Hebrews 12:23 are the edah and qahal, the words Jesus actually spoke or their Aramaic equivalent in Matthew 16:18 and 18:17.)

According to *Jesus*, toward the end, just before the rapture, there will be no great revival except by the antichrist. The true believers will be few and far between. Did not *Jesus ask,*

"Nevertheless, when the Son of Man comes will he really find faith on the earth?"

If what you have been trusting and have leaned upon for your salvation seems to be shaking and not up to the task of these terrible times and what is yet to come, it is probably revealing its man-made pedigree. If it is man-made, it will fall. Do not trust it for your salvation. Instead join the thronging crowd, of which *The Scriptures* speak, that have answered *the call of God* and are *entering mount Zion and the City of the Living God.*

"But you have come to Mount Zion and to the city of the living God, the heavenly Jerusalem, to an innumerable company of angels, to the general assembly and church of the first born who are registered in heaven, to God the judge of just men made perfect, to Jesus, the mediator of the new covenant and to the blood of sprinkling that speaks better things than the blood of Abel. See that you do not refuse Him who speaks.

For if they did not escape who refused Him who spoke on earth, much more shall we not escape if we turn away from Him who speaks from heaven, whose voice then shook the earth; but now He has promised, saying 'yet once more I shake not only the earth, but also heaven."

Now this "yet once more" indicates the removal of those things that are being shaken, as of things that are made, that the things which cannot be shaken may remain. Therefore, since we are receiving a kingdom which cannot be shaken, let us have grace, by which we may serve God acceptably with reverence and godly fear. For our God is a consuming fire.

The Last Command

The last command and promise of Christ that many a living man of faith will be privileged to receive and obey is found in *Luke 21:28.* On that day of redemption, banishing all of his fear by the power of his overcoming trust in his Overcoming Lord, the elect will be saved by his steadfast faith. This faith, this conviction that the Lord possesses the will and power to keep His promise, on time, will strengthen his feeble knees. He will not waiver. He will not run. He will not hide. He will not flee to the Mountains of Judea because the commands to do so are for other times, long past and yet to come, but not for this Day.

The last command is this: *"Now when these things begin to happen look up and lift up your heads; for your redemption draws near."*

The Situation in the Middle East Today and in All of the World and Its Soon Resolution.

Understanding the truth in *Matthew 24* and *Luke 21* destroys the false premises of the parties of these times by setting out the true history of the last days. If you will read *Matthew 24* and *Luke 21* carefully, you will immediately see that the major themes and events up to 70 AD, including the destruction of Jerusalem in that year, are accurately prerecorded in *Luke 21 verses 12 through 24a.*

The second half of Verse 24 then describes the fate of the Jewish people and their relationship to Jerusalem for a period of time that spans the better part of two millennia, up until June 1967. According to *the words of Jesus,* all of these events prerecorded in *verses 12 through 24* must occur before the signs of *verses 10 and 11* which foreshadow the beginning and the end of the final days of trouble can even begin.

The events that are prerecorded in *verses 12 through 19* were actually experienced by the early church and are fully documented in *The Book of the Acts of the Apostles* and other *New Testament writings.* The fulfillment of *verses 20 through the first half of verse 24* was accomplished during the wars between the Jews and the Romans from 67 AD until the 9th of Av 70 AD and the days immediately following. These events are recorded in great detail in the undisputed work of Josephus, *The Wars of the Jews.*

The last half of verse 24 was fulfilled in History from 9 Av 0070 AD to 7 June 1967 AD and is recorded in the history of every nation to which the Jews were driven and in the annals of the modern state of Israel from its declaration of independence on 14 May 1948 to the present hour, especially the events of the Six Day War in June 1967 and more specifically to the Seventh of June when a patrol of Moshe Dayan's young conquering Davids raised the Israeli flag over the Dome of the Rock on the Temple Mount.

However, a shadow of uncertainty remains. Twenty-four hours later Dayan ordered the flag struck and turned the administration of the Temple Mount over to the Waqf, the Muslim entity for overseeing the holy places under the supposed sovereignty of the Jewish Nation. However, this supposed sovereignty of the Jews has been covertly challenged these many years with creeping impositions of the Waqf, culminating recently with total disregard of the terms of their "lease"– even denying Jewish prayers there.

Not only this, they have undertaken unilateral, unauthorized and unsupervised excavations on the Mount in complete rejection of Jewish interests, much less authority or sovereignty. Ariel Sharon made a point of publicly going on the Temple Mount where any Jew should be able to go. This brought about the reaction of the current intifada in which hundreds have died and which brought about the electoral overthrow of the Barak government.

Question: Does the Gentile boot of *Luke 21:24* still trample Jerusalem because the Waqf currently controls the Temple Mount? Maybe, but probably not. The prophesy of Jesus was of Jerusalem, not just the Temple. The times are ripe. We shall see.

Understanding *Luke 21:12* sets in sure order the events of these final days. This understanding will destroy the hopes of the Palestinian Authority to claim Jerusalem. It will also show them the horrible end they personally face as they play out their role, whatever it may be, as instruments of God in their participation in the final breaking of the *people of God.*

Understanding the historical significance of *Luke 21:12* and how it sets the fulfillment of the devastation prophesied in *Matthew 24:7–28 (and Daniel 12, Zechariah 14, and on and on)* in our immediate future, places the Prayer for the Peace of Jerusalem in its proper perspective.

Jerusalem will be devastated one more time; the Holy People will finally be broken as declared in Daniel 12. The remnant, those who say, *"Blessed is He who comes in the Name of the Lord."* will be redeemed from utter destruction by the triumphant return of the Messiah. This remnant will come out of a people that will suffer more than even those of the holocaust. *Jesus, Himself,* will personally destroy the antichrist, judge the nations and have Satan bound.

Christians should not falsely comfort and mislead non-believing Jews, *precious in the sight of God*, by an unqualified prayer for the peace of Jerusalem, but should instead blast out the clear note of the *shofar* (not uncertain tones in the time of battle which leads only to destruction) that the Jews now face death and destruction far worse than the Holocaust. Don't repeat the mantra of "Never Again" if you believe *Jesus'* declaration in *Luke 21:12* and heed its event-ordering significance.

Instead you must cry out, *"Repent and turn to Jesus, your only hope for redemption before it is too late."* For *He* will be calling *His* own out of the caldron very soon, and then worse than the holocaust will fall upon those trapped here below, not just the Jews in Judea, but all over the world, Jews and Gentiles alike.

Indeed, pray for the peace of Jerusalem, but only in the light of the sure knowledge of the return of *Jesus, the Messiah. He* will come at *His appointed hour,* and after the final battle there will be peace in Jerusalem and all over the world for a thousand years. We need to pray that we do not fall into temptation, but remain faithful, waiting for *His appointed time and actions.*

Tell the Jews that Jesus is the Messiah and that He is coming. Tell them to repent and hasten to kiss the Son while there is still time, before the day of grace ends and the night comes.

If they miss His call this time, He will return for them, one more time—seven years later, and then He will fight the Battle of Jerusalem for them. He will win and He will bring peace.

The Rapture

But on the *day of the Rapture*, which is all but upon us, *the believer* is not instructed to fight or to flee, but only to look up and lift up his head because his redemption draws near. The believers will be saved, not by the arm of flesh, but by the power of God.

Tell the Arabs, the Muslims, and the rest of the world that they are also dearly beloved of God, *That Jesus is the Messiah and that He is coming.* Tell them to repent and to hasten to kiss the Son while there is still time before the day of grace ends and the night comes.

These are His Words. This is His promise. It is written.

Those who cannot yet trust these words for their salvation on that day simply do not yet know and believe the promises and the power of the living God. I shake as I write this. Do I yet know the living God? Do I really trust Him? If I do stand *on that day or in this day,* it will be by His strength alone, not by mine. Our salvation is not, and will not be, by our strength, knowledge, wisdom or holiness, But by His love and faithfulness. We must begin immediately to prepare our hearts and minds to be ready to receive this salvation. *He has already, and will always, provide the way.*

Until He Comes

He who did not spare His Own Son, but delivered Him up for us all, how shall He not with Him also freely give us all things. Who shall bring a charge against God's elect? Who shall separate us from the Love of Christ? Shall Tribulation, or distress, or persecution, or famine, or nakedness, or peril, or sword: As it is written: "For Your sake we are killed all day long; we are accounted as sheep for the slaughter." Yet in all these things we are more than conquerors through Him who loved us. For I am persuaded that neither death, nor life, nor angels nor principalities nor powers, nor things present nor things to come, nor height nor depth, nor any other created thing, shall be able to separate us from the Love of God which is in Christ Jesus our Lord.

O live in us Lord Jesus and save us now and forever.

Hosanna!

Now when these things begin to happen, look up and lift up your heads because your redemption draws near.

Come quickly, Lord Jesus.

Maranatha!